"Information Systems Unraveled: Exploring the Core Concepts"

GoodMan, Volume 1

Patrick Mukosha

Published by Patrick Mukosha, 2023.

Title: "Information Systems Unraveled: *Exploring the Core Concepts*"

A **GLOSSARY** of the most widely used Information Systems Concepts.

Abstract

"Information Systems Unraveled: *Exploring the Core Concepts*" is an invaluable resource that delves into the intricate world of Information Systems (IS) through a comprehensive glossary of key terms and concepts. Authored with meticulous attention to detail, this book serves as a compass for both novices and experts in the realm of IS, offering a clear and concise guide to the essential principles that underpin modern information management.

The book acts as a linguistic bridge, connecting readers to the language of Information Systems by providing succinct explanations for a wide array of terms. It is a testament to the authors' expertise in the field, as they curate a diverse collection of concepts that encapsulate the fundamental building blocks of IS.

Notably, the glossary covers a spectrum of topics that span data management, systems architecture, software development, security protocols, and beyond. This wide-ranging scope mirrors the multidisciplinary nature of Information Systems, making the book an invaluable tool for students, professionals, and enthusiasts from various backgrounds.

"Information Systems Unraveled: *Exploring the Core Concepts*" is not just a glossary; it's a guide that empowers readers to navigate the complex world of IS terminology. Through its comprehensive coverage, user-friendly structure, and real-world relevance, the book is destined to become an essential companion for anyone seeking to enhance their understanding of Information Systems and harness its transformative power.

Dr. Patrick C. Mukosha
August, 2023.

Trademarks

All terms mentioned in this book that are known to be trademarks or service marks have been appropriately capitalized. The Author and the publisher cannot attest to the accuracy of this information. Use of a term in this book should not be regarded as affecting the validity of any trademark or service mark.

Warning and Disclaimer

Every effort has been made to make this book as complete and as accurate as possible, but no warranty or fitness is implied. The information provided in this book is on as is basis. The Author and the Publisher shall have neither liability nor responsibility to any person or entity with respect to any loss or damage arising from the use the information contained in this book.

Editorial

Author: Patrick Chisenga Mukosha PhD
Graphics Editor: Satish Kumar Raju

"INFORMATION SYSTEMS UNRAVELED: EXPLORING THE CORE CONCEPTS"

Abend

Abend, which is short for abnormal end, refers to a task or program that ends abruptly. An error message detailing the last operation of the application and the file or memory location where the problem took place is displayed once an ABEND occurs.

Abort

Abort is a term used to denote stopping a process or command in a computer. Usually, an abort is implemented when there has been a mistake or when a task cannot or shouldn't be finished. For instance, you can force a software to close and try opening it again if it stops responding while it is running on your computer.

Absolute Address

An absolute address, often referred to as a direct address, machine address, or actual address, is a precise memory location used by hardware and software. They are used to store data in a certain place so that it can be retrieved more conveniently in the future. The identification of a unique storage location in the computer system (the address) that is permanently assigned by the machine designer. For example, disk drive no. 2, sector no.24, and byte no. 1,650 are absolute addresses. The computer must be given absolute addresses to reference its memory and peripherals.

Absolute Language

A language made up of machine addresses and machine operation codes, i.e., a language using the exact location where the operand is to be found or stored. Synonymous with machine language.

Accelerator

A hardware or software program that aims to boost the computer's overall performance. For instance, a 3D graphics accelerator may do tasks that would otherwise be burdensome for other computer components because it has its own GPU (graphics processing unit) and

RAM. A download accelerator is another excellent example that may be installed to aid increase download speeds.

Access Control Systems

Any system intended to limit user access to a computer system in accordance with predetermined criteria is known as an access control system, or ACS. For instance, on the majority of computers, users must enter a proper name and password in order to log in. These users can only access, create, and edit a limited number of files and directories in the file system after they log in. Multiple users can access a single system using access control while still ensuring the confidentiality and privacy of each user's files. It lessens the possibility that the operating system may malfunction by safeguarding crucial system data from being modified or tampered with.

Access Method

The manner in which records are retrieved from a file.

Access time

The time required to begin and complete the read and write function on a specified block of data. Memory *access time* is the time it takes for a character in memory to be transferred to or from the processor. Disk *access time* is an average of the time it takes to position the read/write head over the requested track.

Activate

Generally speaking, the word "activate" refers to turning something on. For instance, the phrase "product activation" refers to the process of using a serial number, product key, or other unique ID number to activate a piece of software or a game. Software activation with Microsoft Windows or Windows-compatible programs verifies legal ownership and makes the program usable. Before using a piece of software without restrictions, it must first be enabled. You need a legitimate product key in order to activate Windows or installed applications. Microsoft Windows product keys can be found printed on the side of the machine chassis or on a sticker attached to the installation disk.

Active Directory

The service AD (Active Directory), which was formerly known as NTDS, is kept in the NTDS.DIT file. It offers administrators and users a streamlined approach to manage network resources, sites, services, and users. Although it had been demonstrated on Windows NT in 1999, it was first offered in Microsoft Windows 2000. Through the MMC (Microsoft Management Console), the Active Directory functionality is frequently monitored and controlled.

Active Partition

A hard drive partition designated as the bootable partition housing the operating system is known as an active partition. On each hard drive, only one partition can be designated as a bootable or active partition. The active partition, for instance, is the one that contains Windows if you are using Microsoft Windows.

Access Point

An access point is a wireless receiver for connecting wirelessly to a network or the Internet, also known as a base station and wireless router. Both Wi-Fi and Bluetooth devices can be referred to by this phrase. A Linksys wireless access point router is depicted in the image; to boost the signal, it makes use of several antennas.

Administrator

An Administrator, alternatively called an *Admin*, administrator, and gatekeeper, root is a super-user account on a computer or network and has complete control. Person in charge of controlling computer users and system settings. When referring to a Unix and Linux computer, this user is often known as *root*. On a Windows computer and on a network, this user is often called an *administrator*. However, each of these terms is interchangeable. When dealing with computers, there can be many different administrators in a company. Listed below are a few examples of the different administrators a company may employ.

Types of network administrators:

⬦ System Administrator (sysadmin) - Individual responsible for managing the users and system settings of computers.

⬦ DBA (Database Administrator)

⬦ IT, LAN, or Network Administrator

⬦ Linux Administrator - Individual responsible for Linux systems.

Address
A number of a particular memory or peripheral *storage location*. Like post office boxes, every byte of memory and every sector on a disk have their own unique address. After a program has been written, it is translated into machine language that references actual addresses in the computer.

Address Register
A register in which the address is stored. It is a *high-speed circuit* that holds the address of data to be processed or of the next instructions to be executed. A section of the computer's memory used to track memory location. A list of various address registers is provided below. Memory address register, or MAR for short, is a parallel load register that holds the following manipulatable memory address. For instance, the address that will be read or entered next. The destination memory address register is called DMAR. The source memory address register is known as SMAR.

Advanced Persistent Threats (APT)

Advanced Persistent Attackers may infiltrate critical data while purposefully avoiding discovery by the organization's security professionals if they get unauthorized access to a network and go unnoticed for a long time. APTs are often launched against nation states, major corporations, or other extremely valuable targets since they require sophisticated attackers and significant effort.

ADSL

The abbreviation ADSL stands for *Asymmetric Digital Subscriber Line*, also known as *asymmetric DSL*. Due to its two-way bandwidth being split into a large portion for upstream transfers and a small portion for downstream transfers, ADSL is asymmetric. A larger download transfer rate, frequently up to 6.1 megabits per second, is produced by the smaller upstream.

Affiliate Program

A *business or website that refers customers* to other establishments or websites in exchange for payment. The payment could come in the form of a bonus or a portion of what the customer spends.

Algorithm

A *defined process or set of ordered steps for solving a problem*, such as a mathematical formula or the instructions in a program. An algorithm is a solution to a problem that satisfies the requirements listed below. The word algorithm is derived from the name of the mathematician Muhammad ibn-Musa Al-Khowarizmi.

- Anything that always succeeds and is functional.
- A set of guidelines, steps, or a formula that addresses a challenge.
- Can be validated.

Alphabetic Character

"INFORMATION SYSTEMS UNRAVELED: EXPLORING THE CORE CONCEPTS"

An alphabetic character is any character that belongs to the set of letters; ABCDEFGHIJKLMNOPQRSTUVWXYZ and the space (^) character.

Alphanumeric

Pertaining to a character set that contains both letters and numerals, and usually other special characters.

Analog

Pertaining to data in the form of continuously variable physical process or devices that operate on such data. Analog devices monitor conditions, such as movements, temperature and sound, and convert them into analogous or mechanical patterns. For example, an *analog watch* represents the planet's rotation with the rotating hands on the watch face.

Any of the following examples of analog can be used:

a. *An analog signal's graph*: An electronic communication that uses analog technology sends signals with variable frequencies. Analog signals are best represented as graphs, as opposed to digital signals, which convey a binary value, such as ON or OFF. The equipment can manage information that is constantly changing, such as voltage, current, and waves, thanks to analog methods.

b. *VHS cassette tape*: A mechanical or electronic equipment that does not employ digital signals is referred to as an analog device. Analog technologies transmit information like sound or images by storing it on a physical media like film, tape, or vinyl, unlike current computers that share binary, numerical information.

Analog Computer

A computer that accepts and process infinitely varying signals, such as voltage fluctuations or frequencies. A *Thermometer* is the best example of an analog computer. A continuously varying change of temperature causes a metal bar to bend correspondingly (contrast with *Digital*).

Analysis

Breaking something down into its fundamental pieces.

Android

Any of the following may be referred to as Android:

a. A robot with a striking resemblance to a person is called an android.

b. Andy Rubin created the company in October 2003, and on August 17, 2005, Google purchased it. An open software stack including an operating system, middleware, and apps, Android is a free Linux-based platform. On November 5, 2007, Google launched the first version of it for mobile platforms. On September 23, 2008, T-Mobile's G1 phone (HTC Dream) became the first phone running Google Android to be made available to the general market. Apple iOS, a proprietary operating system and platform used on the Apple iPhone, is fiercely competitive with Android.

ANSI (American National Standards Institute)

A non-profit, privately funded membership organization, composed of representatives from industrial firms, technical societies, consumer organizations, and government agencies. *Information technology standards* pertaining to the analysis, control and distribution of information, which includes programming languages, electronic data interchange (EDI), telecommunications and physical properties of diskettes, cartridges and magnetic tapes. E.g. ANSI COBOL and ANSI C are the ANSI-endorsed versions of COBOL and C. Such languages conform to the standards (reserved words, syntax, rules) as set forth by ANSI.

Application

"INFORMATION SYSTEMS UNRAVELED: EXPLORING THE CORE CONCEPTS"

A *specific use of a computer.* E.g. Payroll, inventory and accounts receivable are business applications. Synonymous with application program or software package. Word-processing, spreadsheets and business graphics are applications. Often refers to the running program and the files and databases that are being worked on.

Application Program

Standard and frequently used programs that are tailored to a user's vocational needs. These may be supplied to the user by the manufacturer, purchased from a software house, or written by the user himself.

Archie

Archie is another type of search engine on the Internet. *Archie is a software program*, developed at McGill University, Montreal, Canada, *that searches the indexes of public-access computers* (computers that permit "anonymous FTP") for a keyword that you specify. Only file names and computer subdirectory names are searched, not the text of the actual documents. Archie returns to you a list of the matches it finds. If a particular file interests you, you can log onto the computer where it resides and use anonymous FTP to copy it to your PC.

Archie clients query a single database that contains the locations of various files by filename. This is useful when you wish to know the location of a specific file or program so you can retrieve it using FTP. Although the searches are limited to a file's name rather than a file's content, Archie provides the ability to search the largest number of information sources of any of the information access systems.

Arithmetic Logic Unit (ALU)

The arithmetic logic unit is a major component of the processor and performs all the arithmetic and logic operations in the computer. To carry out its operations, the ALU uses some special and dedicated registers like the *accumulator*; which holds one of the operands before the operations are carried out and it holds the results of the operations. The *arithmetic operations* include; division, multiplication, conversions of numbers, addition, and subtraction. The *logical operations* include; AND, OR, ROTATIONS and NEGATIONS.

Arm

An access mechanism that supports one or more head assemblies for read/write functions on a disc. An arm may be either stationary or movable.

Array

An ordered arrangement of data elements. A one-dimensional array is called a *vector*. A two-dimensional array is called a *matrix*. Most programming languages have the ability to store and manipulate arrays in one, two or more dimensions.

ASCII (American Standard Code for Information Interchange)

Pronounced "ask-ee", is a uniform code in which alphabetic, numeric, and special characters plus several special symbols, are represented by 8-bit configurations. A binary code for data that is used in communications, most mini-computers, and all microcomputers.

Assemble

To prepare an object language program from a *symbolic language* program by substituting machine operation codes for symbolic operation codes and absolute addresses for symbolic addresses.

Assembler

A computer program that operates on symbolic input data to produce machine instructions (machine *code*). An Assembler generally translates input symbolic codes into machine instructions, item by item, and produces, as output, the same number of instructions or constants that were defined in the input symbolic codes. Contrast with a *compiler*, which is used to translate a high-level language, such as COBOL or C into assembly language first and then into machine code.

Assembly Language

"INFORMATION SYSTEMS UNRAVELED: EXPLORING THE CORE CONCEPTS"

A programming language that is one step away from machine language. Each assembly language statement is translated into one machine instruction by the assembler. Programmers must be well versed in the computer architecture, and, unless well documented, assembly language programs are difficult to maintain. Assembly languages are hardware dependent; there is a different language for each CPU series.

Asynchronous

Characterizing different time intervals between events or occurrences. Unsynchronized events, for example, the time interval between event X and Y is not the same as Y and Z.

Asynchronous Data Transmission

The *transmission of data in which each character is a self-contained unit with its own start and stop bits and the intervals between characters may be uneven*. It is the common method of transmission between a computer and a modem, although the modem may switch to synchronous transmission to communicate with the other modem.

Authentication

During system access, the identity of users and other entities is confirmed by *authentication*. Identity can be established via passwords, biometric techniques, and multi-factor authentication (MFA). Authentication is the act of asking a person, piece of software, or piece of hardware for credentials in order to confirm their identity or demonstrate that they are who or what they say they are is known as authentication. Credentials (such as username and password, fingerprints, certificates, or one-time passcodes) are frequently needed for authentication. *AuthN* is a common abbreviation for authentication. Authentication ensures that users or other entities attempting to access a system are who they claim to be. It entails verifying credentials such as biometrics, security tokens, and passwords.

With multi-factor authentication (MFA), users must submit multiple pieces of identification to prove their identities, such as:

Something they possess, such as a security token or badge.

Something they are aware of, like a password.

A biometric (fingerprint or facial) characteristic of them.

With single sign-on (SSO), users only need to confirm their identity once to access a variety of resources that use that same identity. After authentication, the IAM system serves as the user's source of identity truth for all other resources. It eliminates the requirement for multiple, independent target system sign-ons.

Authorization

Authorization controls the degree of access that users who have successfully authenticated have to a system. Common authorization schemes include role-based access control (RBAC) and attribute-based access control (ABAC). A user, computer, or software component's authorization verifies that they have been given permission to access a certain resource. AuthZ is an abbreviated form of authorization. Authorization establishes the degree of access given to users who have successfully authenticated. Users can only access resources and take activities that are authorized by their roles and permissions thanks to this approach.

Auxiliary Storage

A *secondary storage device*, also known as external memory, secondary memory, or auxiliary storage, is a non-volatile storage medium that preserves data until it is erased or replaced. Compared to primary storage, secondary storage is roughly two orders of magnitude less expensive. As a result, supplementary storage to a primary, quicker PCIe SSD may be a hard drive or an additional, slower SSD (solid-state drive). Off-line storage, however, is a subset of secondary storage because they both have the same function and do not communicate with the CPU directly.

- An Illustration Of Secondary Storage:
- Disk Drive

- Tape Drive
- The Solid-State Drive
- Compact Disc (CD)
- Thumb Drive
- An SD Card
- Digital Versatile Disc (DVD)
- A Floppy Disk (Though no-longer used)

Availability

Data availability guarantees that data and services are available when they are required. Denial-of-service (DoS) attacks can interfere with availability and significantly affect enterprises. In order to improve availability, load balancing, redundancy, and robust network design are employed.

B

Backbone

A computer network's backbone is the area that transmits the majority of its traffic at fast speeds. Large networks or organizations frequently have a backbone connecting them. On October 29, 1969, UCLA and SLI established the first Internet backbone. Today, the Internet has numerous sizable backbones that carry the majority of traffic throughout the globe. Numerous of these backbones are managed by telecommunications firms in the United States, including AT&T, Bell South, Congent, Qwest, Level 3, MCI/Worldcom, Sprint, and Time Warner.

Backup

A *backup* is a copy of crucial information that is kept in a different location so that it may be restored if it is lost or corrupted. Depending on how frequently the data changes, how valuable it is, and how long it takes to complete the backup, data should be backed up at intervals.

For instance, a business with rapidly changing client records might back up their data every several hours. On redundant RAID drives, which assist secure the data even in the event of a disk failure, even more delicate data, such as bank information, may be kept. There are numerous methods and storage options available today for information backup and data storage. To back up your data, some common methods are CD-R, DVD-R, USB thumb drives, external devices, and the cloud.

Data on a hard drive could be corrupted or destroyed if the hard disk fails, and a computer could crash at any time. Data on the computer may be lost if hardware or the machine malfunction. To prevent data loss and make sure you can recover any vital files if necessary, all important files should be backed up.

Bandwidth

The *measurement of computer's transmission capacity or communications channel*, usually measured in cycles per second or Hertz. Pure digital transmission is measured in bits or bytes per second.

Baiting

Baiting is when a threat actor places a physical device that is infected with malware, such as a USB drive, where the target may discover it, they successfully fool the victim into utilizing the malicious device. The target unintentionally installs the infection when they plug the device into their PC.

Barebone

A computer system that is *barebones* is one that only has the necessary parts to function, which helps to keep the cost of the system as a whole cheap. The parts that are frequently found in a basic computer are listed below.

- Case (chassis)
- Power source
- Motherboard (often with built-in audio or video).
- Memory
- Visual card
- Audio card

Rarely are extra parts like a computer monitor, wires, a keyboard, a mouse, and other external parts included. This word can also apply to computers that just have a motherboard or case because every computer maker is distinct.

Base

A number base. A *quantity used implicitly to define some system of representing numbers by positional notation*. The multiplier in a numbering system. In a decimal system (base 10), each digit position is worth 10x the position to its right. In a binary system (base 2), each digit is worth 2x positions on its right.

Base Address

The *location in memory where the beginning of a program is stored*. The relative address from the instruction in the program is added to the base address to derive the absolute address. The address contained in an index register.

BASIC (Beginners All-purpose Symbolic Instruction Code)

John Kemeny, Mary Keller, and Thomas Kurtz created the first BASIC at Dartmouth College, where it was initially released on May 1, 1964. Beginner's All-purpose Symbolic Instruction Code, or BASIC, is a simple-to-understand programming language that was well-liked between 1970 and 1980. Although it is not used to create programs anymore, BASIC is nevertheless occasionally used to aid in the instruction of programming concepts.

Although BASIC is *no longer frequently utilized*, its newer iterations, like Visual Basic, are still well-liked and employed.

Batch File

Any of the following may be referred to as a batch file:

Batch document: A *batch file or batch job* is a collection of commands that are executed sequentially, frequently without the involvement of the user. A batch file is kept as a file with a.bat file extension on a computer running a Microsoft operating system, such as Windows. Other operating systems might define a batch job in a shell script that has a set of commands that are to be run sequentially.

Batch files are used to execute many processes simultaneously, load applications, and carry out routine or repeated tasks. A batch job could be used, for instance, to back up files, examine log files, perform many calculations or diagnostics, or perform any other task that calls for running multiple commands. Without the user's involvement, a batch job can complete several tasks, freeing up the user's time for other duties.

The Recovery Console command known as batch runs many commands. For detailed information about this command, visit the batch command page.

Batch Processing

Data processing in which a number of similar input data items are grouped together and processed during a single machine run with the same program for operating convenience and efficiency.

Batch processing, often known as a batch system, is a method of processing data that occurs in one big group rather than individually. Batch processing is frequently used to save system resources and allow for any changes to be made before processing.

As an illustration, a bank might batch process all of its transactions once every hour as opposed to processing each one individually. All of your emails may be kept in Microsoft Outlook's Outbox, which is processed every few minutes and gives you the option to modify or delete before sending.

Baud

Named after Jean-Maurice-Emile Baudot, a French engineer who was the first to gauge the speed of telegraph transmissions. A *baud or baudrate* today refers to the quantity of frequencies or voltages sent over a line each second.

The current standard *Baudrate* settings are 9600, 19200, 57600, and 115200.

Baud Rate

A *unit of transmission speed equal to the number of signal changes in one second.* The relationship of bauds to bits-per-second depends on the data set's design. In some data sets, 1,400 bauds are equivalent to 1,400 bits-per-second, a one-to-one relationship. In other data sets, the baud rate may be 1/2 or 1/3 of the bit-per-second rate.

Benchmark

A *benchmark test* evaluates the efficiency of computer hardware, software, or both. These tests provide comparisons between the performance potential of various items. When comparing benchmarks, the component, software, or entire machine is faster if the value of the results is higher. The image displays a CrystalMark computer benchmark example along with the overall ratings of each of its component parts.

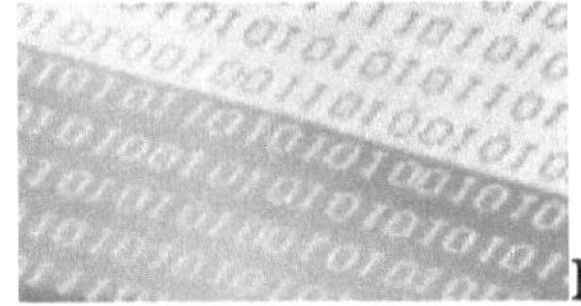 **Binary**

Meaning *two*. Relating to, being, or belonging to a system of numbers having two as its base. The fundamental principle behind digital computers. All input to the computer is converted into binary numbers made up of the two digits 0 and 1 (bits).

Gottfried Leibniz created the *base-2* number system known as binary, which only has two digits or numbers: 0 (zero) and 1 (one). All binary code, which writes digital data like the computer processor instructions used with your everyday gadgets, is based on this numbering scheme.

In binary, the 0s and 1s stand for OFF or ON, respectively. In a transistor, a "0" denotes the absence of electricity and a "1" denotes the presence of electricity. Calculations are possible because numbers are physically represented in the computer in this way. We go into more detail about this idea in our section on how to interpret binary numbers.

For the following reasons, binary is still the most used language for computers and is utilized with electronics and computer hardware:

The most effective method for controlling logic circuits is binary.

It has a clean, sophisticated design.

Only the states of "on" and "off" can be safely maintained by the switches used by current computers.

The binary 0 and 1 approach instantly determines if an electrical signal is on (true) or off (false).

An electrical signal is less sensitive to electrical interference when just two states are spaced widely apart.

Magnetic media's positive and negative poles can be converted to binary very quickly.

BCD (Binary-Coded Decimal)

Describing *a notation in which the individual decimal digits are represented by a pattern of four bits* e.g., the number 12 is represented as 0001 0010 for 1 and 2, respectively. In pure binary notation, twelve is represented as 1100.

BIT (BInary DigiT)

A *single digit in a binary number (1 or 0)*. Within the computer, a bit is physically a memory cell (made up of transistors or one transistor and a capacitor), a magnetic spot on disk or tape or a pulse of high or voltage traveling through a circuit. A group of bits make up storage units in the computer, called characters, bytes, or words, which are manipulated as a group. The most common storage unit is the byte, which is made up of eight bits and equivalent to one alphanumeric character.

BIOS

The BIOS, also known as *Basic Input/Output System*, is a ROM chip present on motherboards that enables you to access and configure your computer system at the most fundamental level. The BIOS contains instructions on how to load the most fundamental pieces of hardware. It includes a POST (Power-On Self-Test) test that assists in determining whether the computer satisfies the prerequisites for successfully booting up. A series of beeps that indicate a computer issue can be heard if the POST is not successfully completed by the machine.

The following are the main functions of a BIOS:

Before loading the operating system, POST is used to test the computer hardware and make sure there are no issues. Our POST and beep codes page has further information on the POST.

Locate the operating system using the Bootstrap Loader. The BIOS will hand control over to another operating system if one is found that is capable.

Low-level drivers known as BIOS drivers provide your computer's hardware some fundamental operating control.

A tool called BIOS setup, sometimes known as CMOS setup, allows you to customize hardware settings, including system settings like date, time, and computer passwords.

Biometric

Biometrics is the measuring of a person's biological traits for the purpose of identifying them when it comes to computers and security. A *biometric identification*, for instance, is when a user logs in to a computer or a facility using their voice or fingerprint. This kind of system is more difficult to forge than a password because it is particular to the user. The face, hand, iris, and retina of a person are additional typical biometrics scanning techniques.

A list of every known biometric device used to enter biometric information into a computer can be seen below. This information is a biometric identifier, which can be a physical, chemical, or behavioral trait.

- *Face Scanner*: Biometric face scanners use measurements of a person's face to determine who they are. For instance, the space between a person's chin, eyes, nose, and mouth (interpupillary distance). If these scanners are intelligent enough to differentiate between a person's image and a real person, they can be incredibly secure. For further details on this concept, see our page on facial recognition.

- *Finger Scanner*: A biometric finger scanner, like the one in the image on this page, uses a person's fingerprint to identify them. These are a safe way to identify someone. However, there are a number of ways to trick fingerprint scanners that are inexpensive and less advanced. For instance, on the television program Myth Busters, a phony fingerprint was created using a Gummy Bear goodie.

- *Hand Scanner* - Just like your fingerprint, your hand's palm is distinctively yours. A biometric hand scanner or hand geometry system uses the palm of the hand to identify the subject.
- *Vein Recognition*: A biometric scan of a user's fingertip or palm to identify their veins.
- *Iris Or Retina Scanner*: A biometric iris or retina scanner reads the iris or retina of the subject's eyes to identify them. Because the retina and iris cannot be copied, these scanners offer a more secure biometric authentication method.
- *Signature Verification System*: The shape of your handwritten signature is recognized by a system that verifies signatures as a form of identity.
- *Voice Scanner*: Last but not least, a voice analysis scanner or voice verification device deconstructs a person's voice statistically to identify them. Although these scanners increase security, certain less advanced scanners can be disregarded using a tape recording.

Block

A *group of disk or tape records* that is stored and transferred as a single unit.

Blockchain

A blockchain is a *data structure made up of records, known as blocks, which are linked to one another in a safe manner using cryptography*. It is a decentralized, widely accepted ledger of transactions and forms the basis of cryptocurrencies like bitcoin.

A unique kind of linked list is a blockchain. Each item on the list has a pointer to the item after it in the list as well as its own metadata. You search through a linked list item by item, using the information from one item to find the next, and then repeating the process. This procedure is helpful for organizing data in part because it allows you to combine two lists by changing a single pointer.

Blockchains vary from other types of networks in that they link backward rather than forward. A new block is generated and it references the one before it.

A group of transactions are contained in a block. A "transaction" is a planned shift of data from one state to another. The information could be generic file information or specific information like ownership of money.

A block's transactions are "atomic," which means they cannot be broken up into smaller groups. Either every transaction took place, or nothing did.

The genesis block is the first block made. Every other block eventually ties back to the genesis block, which is the sole block that has no predecessors. Blockchains are frequently pictured as being built vertically, from the bottom up, hence the term "block height," which refers to a block's distance from the genesis block.

After the genesis block, each block has a pointer to the block before it (its "parent"), as well as a hash of that block's header. This hash has unpredictable and distinctive cryptographic characteristics. The blockchain's mathematical properties are what make it resistant to forgery.

The most recent block—also referred to as the chain's "tip," "head," or "top"—must be used as the starting point for each traversal. Then you move backward, one block at a time, "down" the chain.

A block can only reference one "parent" block before it. However, it is possible for many blocks to point to the same parent, which results in a fork in the chain.

The chain's or a fork's tip's top is augmented with new blocks.

As a distributed ledger technology, or DLT, blockchain is effective. There are no private transactions in a distributed ledger; instead, the ledger is publicly shared by all participants. In these transactions, a chain of trust is established through the cryptographic verification that occurs from block to block.

The blockchain is a decentralized, trustworthy record of information because of these characteristics. Blockchain technology enables cryptocurrency owners to transfer money among themselves without the assistance of a centralized financial institution.

Blogger

Any of the following may be mentioned by a blogger:

A *blogger* is someone who creates content for a weblog, also known as a blog. Blogging is a common term for writing in a blog. For instance, you are "blogging" about your day if you maintain a blog on WordPress and write a post about it.

Users can build blogs using the Blogger service. Users can construct web pages that are hosted on the integrated DNS provider, BlogSpot, using a visual interface that doesn't require any code. Pyra Labs launched Blogger on August 23, 1999, and Google now owns it after purchasing the service on February 17, 2003. Any device can access and utilize the Blogger service for free.

Bluetooth

Bluetooth is a computing and telecommunications industry specification that describes how devices can communicate with each other. Bluetooth devices include computers, keyboards and mice, personal digital assistants, and smartphones.

Bluetooth is an RF technology operating at 2.4 GHz and has an effective range of 32 feet (10 meters), varying by power class, a transfer rate of 1 Mbps, and a throughput of 721 Kbps.An example of how Bluetooth could be used is connecting a smartphone to a computer without wires or special connectors. The picture is an example of a USB Bluetooth adapter from SMC. This adapter could be plugged into the USB port to get Bluetooth access on a computer.

Below are some other examples of how Bluetooth is used:

- **Bluetooth speaker** - Speakers that connect to any Bluetooth audio device.
- **Bluetooth headphones** - Headphones that connect to any Bluetooth device.
- **Bluetooth lock** - Door lock that lets you remotely lock and unlock a door.
- **Bluetooth keyboard** and **Bluetooth mouse** - Wireless keyboards and mice.
- **Bluetooth car** - A car with Bluetooth can make hands-free calls in the car.
- **Bluetooth watch** or **Bluetooth health monitor** - Bluetooth wrist devices that transmit data to other devices over Bluetooth.

A *Bluetooth card* is an expansion card installed into a desktop computer to give it Bluetooth capabilities or a stronger Bluetooth signal. In the picture is an example of a PCIe Wi-Fi Card from TP-Link that allows the computer to communicate over Wi-Fi 6 and Bluetooth 5.2. In this example, the card also has antennas not connected directly to the card, which allows the antennas to be better positioned.

BNC Connectors

Any of the following may be referred to as BNC:

A *BNC connector*, also known as a *Bayonet Neill-Concelman connector*, is a style of connector used with coaxial Ethernet wire. The connector is designed in a bayonet fashion, requiring insertion before being rotated and locked into place. On a Token Ring network, this connector is frequently employed. Although more accurately known as the Bayonet Neill-Concelman, BNC is sometimes known as the Bayonet Nut Connector and the British Naval/Navy Connector.

BNC, which stands for bouncer, is a piece of software that relays a user's IRC or FTP communication to their computer through a network in order to protect and conceal them. In order to conceal their

IP address, a user could, for instance, connect to a machine utilizing psyBNC, relay traffic from that source, and connect to an IRC or FTP server. The IP address for the machine that is running the BNC software will be revealed once this is done.

Bookmark

When you find a website that you want to remember and return to later, a bookmark comes in helpful. You may easily visit a website you've bookmarked by creating a shortcut to it. You don't need to search the Internet for that bookmark; you may access it whenever you want to browse the website again.

Any of the following can be referenced by a bookmark:

A *bookmark* is a function that enables you to tag phrases, images, charts, or other items in word processing systems like Microsoft Word so that you may easily discover and examine them later. You may add a bookmark to a chart in a Word document, for instance, if you found the chart to be really helpful. When you need to refer to that chart again in the future, you may open the Word document and use the bookmark to locate it right away.

A *bookmark*, sometimes known as an electronic bookmark, is a way to save the URL of a web page in an Internet browser. The majority of browsers allow you to bookmark the page you're on by hitting Ctrl+D. Click the Bookmark icon (star) icon (or a comparable symbol) to the right of the address bar to bookmark a page with your mouse.

A *bookmark link* is another term for a named anchor when discussing the Internet and HTML.

A *bookmark* is a tool that enables you mark a line in text editors like Notepad++ so you can easily find it later. For instance, you can add and remove a bookmark on the current line in Notepad++ by pressing Ctrl+F2. A tiny blue dot shows next to the line number when it is bookmarked. Pressing F2 will cycle through all of the bookmarked lines in the file once bookmarks have been added. Using bookmarks makes it simple to go through a file with thousands of lines of text or code.

Boolean

A *boolean*, sometimes known as a *bool*, is a data type in computer science that can take on the true or false values. It bears the name George Boole after the English mathematician and logician, whose algebraic and logical frameworks constitute the foundation of all contemporary digital computers.

"BOOL-ee-an" is how you pronounce boolean. Only when referring to Boolean algebra or logic, the word "*Boolean*" should be capitalized. The word "*boolean*" should be spelt with a lowercase b when discussing the data type in computer programming.

Boot

To *start the computer*. Booting the computer helps it get its first instructions. Personal computers have a bootstrap routine in a ROM chip that is automatically executed when the computer is turned on or reset. It searches for the operating system, loads it and the passes control over to it.

Bpi (Bits per Inch)

Used to measure the number of bits stored in a linear inch of a track on a recording surface, such as on a disk or tape.

Bps (Bits per Second)

Used to measure the speed of data transfer in a communication system.

Branch

To depart from the normal sequence of executing instructions in a computer.

Broad Band

High-speed Internet access is made possible by the telecommunications technology known as *broadband*, which uses many channels of active digital signals at once. Broadband can communicate wirelessly over a cellular network or over a physical connection utilizing coaxial, fiber optic, or twisted-pair cable.

Wideband transmission or *high-speed Internet* are other names for broadband, which is also frequently referred to as *BB*. A cable connection or a wireless connection can be used to connect computers in a house or company to broadband. Both of these things, however, require the purchase or rental of a network router from the ISP (Internet service provider). Your LAN (local area network) computers can connect to the Internet thanks to the router.

The PCs at home or at the office connect to the router once it is online. A Cat 5 Ethernet cable is frequently used by computers for wired connections to link the network card within the machine to the router. The router needs to be wireless and configured with a recognized SSID in order to support wireless connections. Once the router is configured, a smartphone, computer, or other device with Wi-Fi functionality can connect to the router's SSID.

In comparison to dial-up, a broadband Internet connection provides a faster, more enjoyable online experience. Web pages load more rapidly, downloads are finished more quickly, and online video streaming is possible with a quicker Internet connection. Users of broadband services can also distribute their connection among several home appliances and laptops. For instance, a router or modem with Wi-Fi capabilities can let all laptops, smartphones, and other Wi-Fi-capable devices in the house share a single broadband connection.

A broadband connection is always active, in contrast to a dial-up connection, which connects only after dialing a number and connecting to another computer.

Browser

A *browser*, often known as a *web browser* or *Internet browser*, is a piece of software used to display and browse content on the World Wide Web. Links between these content items, which include images, videos, and web pages, are used, and URIs (Uniform Resource Identifiers) are used to categorize them. This page serves as an illustration of how a browser can be used to read a web page.

Over the years, a wide variety of web browsers have emerged and disappeared. Tim Berners-Lee created the first, initially known as World-Wide-Web (later renamed Nexus), in 1990. NCSA Mosaic, however, was the first and most popular graphical browser that contributed to the growth of the Internet.

Your machine is allowed to have more than one (or all) of the aforementioned browsers installed as long as it satisfies the browser's system requirements.

Buffer

An internal portion of either a computer, terminal, or peripheral that temporarily stores data while it is being processed.

Bulletin Board

A *system with a computer, modem, and phone line that acts as a central point for information exchange.* It can be used for electronic mail and for storing files that can be downloaded.

Bus

A *computer bus system is a common channel, or pathway, between hardware devices, either internally between components in a computer or externally between stations in a communication network.* The bus system is composed of electrical connections that move from component to component and so forming a data highway inside the computer for transporting signals. When the bus architecture is used in the computer, the processor(s), memory banks and peripheral control units are all interconnected through the bus. There are three types of buses in the computer, namely data bus, address bus and control bus. The ***data bus*** is used to transfer data from the CPU to other parts of the computer and vice versa. The ***address bus*** is used is used to carry the address numbers which are used to identify each memory location in the computer's memory or identifying particular chips in the computer.

The ***control bus*** is used to carry control signals from the processor to control the operations of the computer. When you plug in a board into one of the expansion slots in your computer, you are effectively plugging into the bus.

Business Continuity

Business continuity refers to the proactive planning and preparation done to guarantee that an organization will be able to carry out its essential business tasks in the event of an emergency. Events can include pandemics, corporate crises, natural catastrophes, workplace violence, or any other occurrence that prevents your organization from operating normally. It's crucial to keep in mind that you should plan and be ready for both incidents that will fully halt operations as well as those that could have a negative influence on services or other functions.

BC focuses on the planning and preparation required to guarantee that a company will be able to carry out its essential business tasks in the event of an emergency. It determines, arranges for, or produces:

- Processes to utilize as a workaround when technology is unavailable.
- How to interact with clients, partners, and other parties to make sure you are giving accurate information and support.
- How to guarantee that clients can still receive services or goods.
- The timing and order necessary to restart business processes.
- How to assist staff members in case of emergency.
- Technology is needed to support corporate operations; disaster recovery (DR) will put recovery measures in place for technology.
- Documentation of the procedures and actions to be followed during an event in order to complete the aforementioned tasks.

- In the event that business locations are affected or unavailable, where and how to relocate people and operations.
- The teams and structure that will be required to manage emergency situations.
- Dependencies of business processes (what or who does each business process rely on to function).
- Regular testing to ensure that strategies and actions are appropriate and will work in a real situation.
- Make sure there will be enough workers at an event to meet both internal and external needs.

Byte

Made up of eight binary digits (bits). The common unit of computer storage from personal computers to mainframes.

PATRICK MUKOSHA

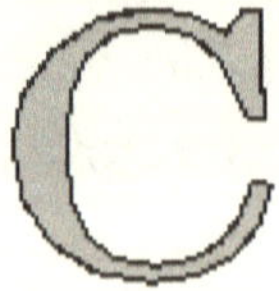

Cable

Any of the following may be referred to as a *cable*:

A *cable*, also known as a cord, connector, or plug, consists of one or more plastic-covered wires used to *transfer power or data between* two or more objects. The power cord for your computer or monitor may resemble the one in the image. One of the countless wires found in and around computers is the power cord.

A *data cable* and a *power cable* are the two basic categories of computer cables. A data cable is a cable that allows devices to communicate with one another. For instance, the DVI, HDMI, or VGA data cable that connects your computer to your monitor enables it to show a picture on the monitor.

There are two main types of computer cables, a data cable and a power cable. A data cable is a cable that provides communication between devices. For example, the data cable (i.e., DVI, HDMI, or VGA) that connects your monitor to your computer allow it to display a picture on the monitor. Other popular examples of data cables include the CAT5, IDE/EIDE, SATA, and USB cables. A power cable is any cable that powers the device. For example, the power cord that connects to your computer and a Molex style cable inside the computer are examples of power cables. Below, is a listing of the most common types of cables found with computers and electronics and examples of devices that use them.

Types of cables:

- AT - Used with early keyboards.
- ATA - Used with hard drives and disc drives.
- Cat 5 - Used with network cards.
- IDE/EIDE - Used with hard drives and disc drives.
- DisplayPort - Used with computer monitors.
- Coaxial - Used with TV and projectors.

- Composite - Used with TV, projectors, and consoles - Also known as RCA cables.
- DVI - Used with monitors, projectors, and other displays.
- eSATA - Used with external drives.
- MIDI - Used with musical keyboards and other equipment.
- Firewire (IEEE-1394) - Used with digital cameras and external drives.
- Parallel - Used with printers.
- HDMI - Used with monitors, projectors, DVD/Blu-ray players, and other displays.
- Mini plug - Used with headphones, microphones, speakers.
- Molex - Power cable used inside your computer.
- PS/2 - Used with keyboards and mice.
- S-Video - Used with projectors, digital cameras, and other displays
- VGA/SVGA - Used with monitors and projectors.
- S/PDIF - Used with DVD and surround sound.
- Thunderbolt - Primarily used with Apple displays and devices.
- SATA - Used with hard drives and disc drives.
- SCSI - Used with hard drives, tape drives, and disc drives.
- Serial (RS-232) - Used with a mouse and Modem.
- USB - Used with keyboard, mouse, printer, MP3 players, and thousands of other devices.

Cache memory

Pronounced "*cash*". Cache memory *is reserved portions of high-speed memory, which resides between the processor and the main memory and is used to interface between the slow communicating main memory to the processor, thereby improve performance.* The data and programs that are frequently used are fetched well in advance from main memory and placed in cache memory, and instruction execution and data updating are performed in high-speed memory.

Any of the following may be referred to as a cache:

Cache, *which is pronounced like currency*, is a high-speed access area that is either a reserved area of main memory or a location on the storage device. Memory cache and disk cache are the two primary types of caching. Because most programs regularly access the same data or instructions, memory cache, a component of high-speed static random access memory, is effective. The computer can operate more quickly and effectively by avoiding accessing the slower DRAM by storing as much of this data in SRAM as possible.

When a CPU requests data from memory and finds it already in the cache, the request is referred to as a cache hit. If there is a cache hit, the CPU can virtually instantly access the data. Cache misses, on the other hand, occur when the information is not there in cache. The CPU must wait for the data to be fetched from the slower memory when a cache miss occurs.

While older computers only had L1 cache, modern systems typically have L3 or L2 cache. The Intel i7 processor and its shared L3 cache are demonstrated here.

The *cache feature on Internet browsers* stores website material temporarily. The web browser can increase efficiency by loading data from your disk rather than the Internet if it is ever needed again by caching this information. A web page and all of its files are typically transferred to the browser's temporary cache on the hard disk each time you access a web page. The browser loads the material from cache rather than downloading the files again if the web page or its resources haven't changed since you last saw them. Cache helps you save time and bandwidth for the website owner, especially if you use a modem.

When IBM unveiled expansions to the System/360 family in 1968, including the Model 85, cache was first introduced. The System/360 Model 85 features the first high-speed cache or buffer memory in the sector. Highly prioritized data is made available from the cache memory at a speed that is 12 times faster than main-core memory.

Calibration

By providing a *measurement instrument* with the knowledge it needs to recognize the context in which it will be used, calibration sets it up. A device's accuracy when collecting data is ensured by *calibration*.

When turned on, a lot of contemporary electronic devices calibrate. For instance, a compass, augmented reality measurement, or other GPS smartphone applications calibrate themselves for a brief period of time by determining their direction in the environment. Other equipment, such as printers, may occasionally show "calibrating" when they are undergoing the calibration procedure to maintain the printer's best performance.

Software for computers may also provide calibration features to adjust its settings in accordance with the hardware. For instance, when running for the first time, high-performance graphics software may go through a calibration procedure to determine how well it will work with the specific hardware on that machine.

While testing, the software might modify its settings and offer the user a recommendation for the best software configuration.

Canned Software

Software that you can buy off the shelf at a store is known as *canned software*, as opposed to software that is custom-made for you and not the ordinary customer.

CAPTCHA

The acronym CAPTCHA is pronounced as *cap-cha*. The CAPTCHA security measure, which stands for **Completely Automated Public Turing Test to Tell machines and Humans Apart**, distinguishes between humans and machines. A CAPTCHA is frequently a text image that has been altered so that only humans can read it, as opposed to the majority of automated computer vision systems. The image serves as a CAPTCHA example.

The visitor can visually recognize the terms "overlooks" and "inquiry" in the image to confirm they are human. A user would not be able to proceed without entering this data onto the web page. Unfortunately, visitors who are blind or have vision problems have trouble using CAPTCHAs since they can't read the letters that are displayed in the image. An audible CAPTCHA will read a message to assist these users in accessing a page that is secured by a CAPTCHA.

Software bots are used to automate repetitive operations like filling out forms to post advertisements on websites. A website will use a CAPTCHA to check whether you are a human or a robot in order to defend itself against these bots. As the user selects the I'm not a robot check box, this protection is carried out by examining the mouse movements and looking for any other anomalies.

Alan Turing developed the idea of the Turing test in 1950, hence the "T" in CAPTCHA. The Turing test involves a person determining which of two speakers is human and which artificial intelligence is by listening to their dialogue. This idea is taken and, as the name suggests, automated by a CAPTCHA.

A group of people, including Manuel Blum, Nicholas J. Hopper, John Langford, Gili Raanan, Eran Reshef, Eilon Solan, and Luis von Ahn, came up with the idea of a CAPTCHA in 1997. In a May 2003 article titled "CAPTCHA: Using Hard AI Problems for Security," they discussed the concept and application of CAPTCHAs. That same year, they also came up with the word "CAPTCHA".

Cathode Ray Tube (CRT)

The vacuum tube used as a display screen in a video terminal or TV. The term is often used to refer to the entire terminal.

CD-ROM (Compact Disc, Read Only Memory)

A CD-ROM, which stands for compact disc read-only memory, is an optical disc with read-only memory that contains audio or software data. They are read via an optical drive, sometimes known as a CD-ROM drive. The CD (compact disc) may be read by CD-ROM devices at speeds ranging from 1x to 72x, which is roughly 72 times quicker than the 1x version. These drives can read and play data CDs, including CD-R (compact disc recordable) and CD-RW (compact disc re-writable) discs, as well as audio CDs, as you might expect.

A DVD (digital versatile disc), either a movie or data DVD, cannot be read by a CD-ROM player. A CD-ROM drive is not made to read the format of a DVD because it differs from a CD. In order to read a DVD, a DVD-ROM drive or newer disc technologies, such as Blu-ray drives, are needed.

Computers that are more recent don't have disc drives (CD drives) anymore. Take a look at the front of your computer to see if it has a CD drive. A CD reader tray or slot should be located on the front of the computer. whether a CD drive is not visible to the naked eye, check your computer's disks to see whether your operating system recognizes one.

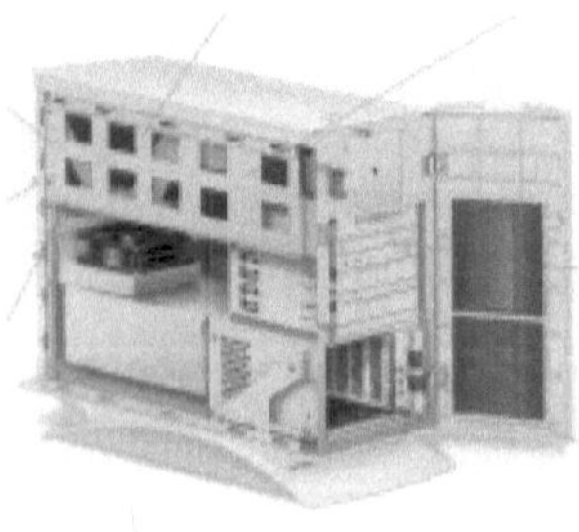

Central Processing Unit (CPU)

The central processor of the computer system contains the internal memory unit (memory), the arithmetic logic unit (ALU), and the input/output control unit (I/O Control). The CPU is basically synonymous with the computer. It is the CPU that controls the operations of the computer, performs the processing and computations, and stores the application software. Within the CPU is the system board (often called the *motherboard*). This board contains the microprocessor, which is responsible for the basic elements of computer processing: arithmetic, logic, and control. The microprocessor is an integrated circuit chip; a dense network of microscopic electrical pathways etched into highly refined sand, or silicon. Adding a co-processor can enhance the performance of motherboards. This works only with applications designed specifically for them. Co-processors can speed up processing time and are especially useful for mathematical calculations.

The motherboard also contains the Random Access Memory (RAM) chips. The RAM is the computer's short-term memory area or the electronic "work space" in which software, programs, and data reside while they are active. When computer operators want to use a certain application or work with certain data, they call it into the RAM where it resides temporarily until it is stored again or until the computer is turned off.

The motherboard cannot always handle all it is asked to do and it is possible to add expansion boards to a computer's CPU. *Expansion boards* are also called daughter boards, adapter boards, or expansion cards. A user can customize a computer by adding expansion boards for color, animation, or sound. They can be used to speed up processing time or increase RAM. Many of these additional capabilities require more than the expansion board. Color, for example, needs a monitor that is capable of displaying color.

The CPU also contains the power supply, which converts electrical currents to a form used by the computer. Some power supplies include surge or spike protectors that guard against damage caused by sudden changes in the electrical supply. A fan cools the power supply while the computer is on.

Chaining

The *capability of one computer program to call another program* for execution following its own execution.

Chad

A piece of paper that is punched out when forming a hole on or notch in a storage medium such as punched tape or cards.

Channel

A *path along which signals can be sent* e.g., data channel, and output channel. Also that part of the output channel, which is accessible to a given reading station.

Character

A single alphabetic letter, numeric digit, or special symbol such as a decimal point or comma. A character is equivalent to a byte, e.g., 5,000 characters take up 5,000 bytes.

Character Recognition

The ability of a machine to recognize printed text. See OCR and MICR.

Chatterbot

A *chatterbot*, also known as a chatbot, is a piece of software or a script created to mimic a discussion between two real people.

Chief Information Officer (CIO)

CIO can be used to describe any of the following:

The most senior executive in an organization who oversees information technology and the management of computer systems is known as the CIO, or chief information officer. The chief information officer reports to the CEO (chief executive officer), CFO (chief financial officer), and COO (chief organizational officer) in a typical organizational hierarchy.

The chief investment officer, or CIO, is a member of the organization who is primarily in charge of deciding how to invest the firm's cash and resources. Typically, a director from the board of directors holds the post.

The JFS filesystem offers an optional feature called concurrent input/output. Files on a JFS drive are no longer write-locked to multiple processes when CIO is enabled. Under normal circumstances, if many processes attempted to write to the same file simultaneously, this might result in inconsistent data. But some programs, like relational databases, can examine the consistency of the data. In certain circumstances, turning on CIO can lower filesystem overhead, enhancing performance in general.

A person in charge of technical innovation within an organization, such as a firm, is known as a CIO, or chief innovation officer. Chief technological innovation officer, CINO, or CTIO are other names for the CIO. Creating new ideas and overseeing the new ideas of other organizational members are responsibilities. The chief innovation office role is crucial to an organization's success.

Circuit

1. A communication channel between two or more points.

2. A set of electronic components that perform a particular function in an electronic system.

Clock

A device that generates signals used for synchronization. An internal timing device.

Clock Speed

The *internal heartbeat and speed of a computer*. The clock circuit uses the fixed vibrations generated from quartz crystal to deliver a steady stream of pulses to the processor. A faster clock will speed up all processing operations provided the computer's circuits can handle the increased speed.

Clone

Any of the following may be referred to as a clone:

One definition of a clone in the context of computer manufacture (and occasionally software development) is a product that closely matches another, successful product. Examples include "IBM clones" or "PC clones" for computers that were "IBM PC compatible". They share the same operating system, extension cards, and aesthetic as IBM PCs. The 1982 release of the Compaq Portable was one of the first IBM clones.

A disk clone is a complete disk or disk partition that has been copied byte for byte. An image file that can be kept in the filesystem or another partition may be used to write the clone directly. Image files can be compressed to save disk space or encrypted to preserve privacy.

Cloud

With computers and the Internet, a *cloud* is a service provided over a network by a collection of remote servers. See our cloud computing page for further information and examples. With the popularity of the cloud, many services and companies also use cloud as part of their company name or product. Below are examples of such terms containing cloud.

A cloud is a service offered across a network by a number of remote servers when it comes to computers and the Internet. Visit our cloud computing page for further details and illustrations. Due to the cloud's growing popularity, numerous services and businesses now incorporate the cloud into the name of their organization or product.

Cloud Computing

The term "*cloud computing*" refers to services delivered across a network by a number of distant servers. This fictitious "cloud" of computers offers vastly spread processing and storage resources that can be accessed by any web-enabled device with an Internet connection. Due of the simplicity of uploading and downloading information, cloud computing is advantageous for businesses, schools, and everyone else. This makes it simple to share information both locally and internationally.

On your computer, smartphone, tablet, or other mobile device, you can access the cloud by using an application (such as the Dropbox app). A website can frequently be used to access cloud computing via your browser. Cloud computing is supported by all modern browsers, including Google Chrome, Microsoft Edge, Apple Safari and Mozilla Firefox.

Data can be retrieved from and delivered to the cloud using the application or browser after it is connected to cloud computing.

Cloud Security

"INFORMATION SYSTEMS UNRAVELED: EXPLORING THE CORE CONCEPTS"

The collection of cybersecurity safeguards used to safeguard infrastructure, data, and applications housed on the cloud is known as *cloud security*. In order to protect cloud environments against unauthorized access, online assaults, and insider threats, security policies, practices, controls, and other technologies, such as identity and access management and data loss prevention systems, must be implemented.

Application, data, and infrastructure security in *cloud environments* are addressed through cybersecurity policies, best practices, controls, and technology. In particular, cloud security works to provide access control, data governance and compliance, disaster recovery, and storage and network protection against internal and external threats. The technology of choice for businesses seeking the flexibility and agility necessary to accelerate innovation and satisfy the demands of today's modern consumers is cloud computing. To ensure that data is secure across online infrastructure, apps, and platforms, a migration to more dynamic cloud environments is necessary.

Cluster

A cluster is *the smallest disk space that will be allocated to a file and can be identified in the File Allocation Table (FAT) as relating to a particular file*, no matter how small it may be. One cluster can only hold one file. However, a large file can be spread over many clusters. A cluster is the smallest group of sectors that can be utilized as a single unit and is composed of one or more sectors. Clusters vary in sizes depending on the disk being used and how the disk was formatted. The actual number of sectors in a cluster is dependent on the type of disk being used.

CMOS

The *CMOS battery. Complementary metal-oxide semiconductor*, or CMOS, is also referred to as a real-time clock, NVRAM (non-volatile random-access memory), or CMOS RAM. Computers have an inbuilt, battery-operated semiconductor chip called CMOS that serves as a data storage device. This data includes your computer's hardware settings and the system time and date. The most typical CMOS coin cell battery (Panasonic CR 2032 3V) used to power the CMOS memory.

The earliest RTC and CMOS RAM device used in early IBM systems, the Motorola 146818 chip, could store 64 bytes of data. The remaining 50 bytes in RAM (random-access memory) were utilized to store system settings after the system clock exhausted 14 bytes of RAM. Nowadays, the majority of computers have merged the settings from the CMOS into the Southbridge or Super I/O chips.

Coaxial Cable

Coaxial cables are used to transmit audio, video, and communications signals. High bandwidths and increased transmission capacity are features of this cable. Coaxial or coax cables are most commonly associated with connecting TVs to cable TV services. However, similar cables are also employed in networks and are what enable a cable modem-based broadband Internet connection.

COBOL (COmmon Business Oriented Language)

A high-level business programming language that has been the primary business application language on minis and mainframes. *COBOL*, initially appeared in 1959, the same year that Grace Hopper, Bob Bemer, and other developers started working on it. The second-oldest high-level programming language, COBOL is still widely used by corporations and the government. The oldest is FORTRAN.

Code

A set of symbols representing rules for handling the flow or processing of information.

Coding

Writing a computer program either in machine code or a high-level language.

Computer Output on Microform (COM)

"INFORMATION SYSTEMS UNRAVELED: EXPLORING THE CORE CONCEPTS"

Also called *Computer Output on Microfilm*; or *Computer Output on Microfiche*. The two types of microform are *microfiche* and *microfilm*. Microfilm is a continuous strip of film containing images formed in frames. Microfiche are small rectangular sheets of film that contain several frames, which are arranged in rows. COM is used in where large volumes of information are required to be stored such as in large libraries and in banks. Therefore, large amount of space can be saved by use of microfilm, and they are relatively cheap. However, special viewing equipment is required to view the information stored on microfilm.

Command

An order given to the computer by the user, which specifies the operation to be performed.

Common Carrier

An organization that provides telecommunications services for public use, such as government operated PTT's.

Communication

Computer-based communication, is the use of computers and telecommunication devices, such as telephones and modems, to send messages. *Electronic mail* (or e-mail) is one popular form. This is the process of transferring the electronic equivalent of a piece of paper from one location to another, perhaps with copies to several addresses or even to a whole mailing list. After receiving the message, people can then respond, again copying their response to others.

Some of the *advantages of computer-based communication* include; the provision of a means to bridge time and distance to facilitate interpersonal communication. It presents the opportunity for as many people as have the need or desire to communicate about a particular subject (or many subjects) to do so without being either physically present in the same location (as in a conventional meeting), or even available at the same time (as in a telephone conference call or a video teleconference).

Thus, computer-based communications enables users to:

Establish a communication line and immediate contacts among users of like interests,

Have a better flow of information,

Get widely involved in ongoing discussions on various topics of interest, without any need for travel, and

Bridge some language barriers, as it is generally easier for people to deal in the written form of unfamiliar languages,

However, there are some problems associated with using computer-based communication. Such communication is a technical reality and is in every-day use in many organizations; however, getting it into place in a new environment can be another matter. Complex economic, social, political, and legal factors will certainly affect the use of the technology and may in some cases present barriers to its successful implementation. The telecommunications systems in many African countries are suffering from deteriorating equipment and inadequate investment. Some forms of computer-based communications can be expensive. In some African countries telecommunications costs are high in relation to other costs, and participation in some computer-based communication activities can require scarce foreign exchange.

To achieve computer-based communication the user needs a computer, a modem, communications software, and access to a telephone line. A system needs the use of data access links (which may be a simple, ordinary telephone or an international packet-switched data network), a computer to act as "host" for the discussion, and a terminal device.

Experience has proven, however, that there are a number of additional factors that contribute to the success of computer-based communication:

"INFORMATION SYSTEMS UNRAVELED: EXPLORING THE CORE CONCEPTS"

There must be a need to communicate: those involved must have something to say to each other and must be willing to say it and pay for it.

Reliable, low-cost, readily available data communication facilities are essential.

Participants must have easy access to a terminal, as the systems work best when accessed directly.

The host system must be reliable, accessible, and easy to use.

A communications advisor must be involved who will help the moderator and participants to start the conference process and keep it moving.

Institutional recognition and support, beyond funding and provision of equipment is needed.

Participation in this type of information exchange must be appreciated as being as valuable as traditional forms of scientific communication.

A leader who is able to fire the imagination of the key participants and funding agencies helps keep the conference moving.

Communication Channel

A telephone line or facility provided by a common carrier.

Communication Protocol

A *set of hardware and software standards for transmitting data* between terminals and computers.

Communication Satellite

An *earth satellite designed to act as a telecommunication radio relay*. Most telecommunication satellites, (other than the Russian ones), are in orbit 22,300 miles above the equator, traveling at the speed of the earth (geosynchronous), so that they appear from the earth to be stationary.

Compare

A fundamental capability of a computer. By comparing one set of data with another, the computer can locate, analyse, select, reorder and make decisions. After comparing the computer can indicate whether the data were equal or which set was greater or less than the other.

Compatibility (Upward or Downward)

The compatibility of a computer program written for a lower level EDP system to be used on a higher-level system, and vice versa.

Compilation Process

The *compiling of a computer program.* The series of events that occur as the source program is translated and assembled into an object program.

Compiler

A software program that translates symbolic input data (from high-level language such as COBOL, and C) into machine code. The compiler usually generates assembly language first then translates the assembly language into machine code.

Computer

A *device capable of accepting data in the form of facts and figures, applying prescribed processes to the data, and supplying the result of these processes as meaningful information.* This device usually consists of input and output devices, storage, arithmetic and logic unit, and control unit. Usually, an automatic, stored machine is implied.

Computer Conferencing

A computer conference *emulates a face-to-face conference where many people meet to discuss an issue of common concern.* Computer conferences include a private *'messaging'* module to simulate the corridor or coatroom discussions that often take place at meetings but they also permit communication among multiple users and allow more flexible treatment of conference comments. In effect, they provide the basis for a location-independent *'virtual meeting'* with an open-ended database of the contributions to the discussion. All those who wish (or need) to participate in a computer conference may do so, each at their own convenience, on their own time schedule, and from their own choice of location.

Computer Output Microfilm (COM)

Machines that create microfilm or microfiche directly from the computer. COM units can be stand alone or online to the computer and receive input the same as data sent to a printer; already formatted with page headers, numbers etc.

Confidentiality

Confidentiality guarantees that only authorized people or organizations can access information. It entails taking precautions to stop unwanted access, disclosure, or leakage of private data. Three popular methods to maintain confidentiality are data classification, encryption, and access controls.

Connector

A flow chart symbol used to indicate the interconnection of two points in a flowchart.

Any cable or wire that links two devices together.

Console

The main operator's terminal on a large computer.

Any display terminal.

Constant

In programming, any data with fixed values within the program. Minimum and maximum amounts, dates, prices, headlines and error messages are examples of constants.

Control Character

A *character whose occurrence in a particular context initiates, modifies, or stops a control operation*, e.g., a character such as line feed, carriage return, and escape, may or may not be printable.

Control Clerk

The control clerks are members of the data processing department and are *responsible for receiving data from the users and finally dispatching the results of the processing*, from the processing department back to the users. When data is received, the control clerks record its details such as date and time it is received in the department, and where it has come from. The data control supervisor forwards the data to the data preparation supervisor, for him to assign batches of data to his data entry operators for entry.

Control Mark (CM)

An l-record block used in magnetic tape processing to indicate the end-of-information, end-of-tape, end-of-file, etc.

Control Register (CR)

A register, which *holds the identification of the instruction to be executed next in the sequence following the current operation*. The register is a counter, which is incremented to the address of the next sequential storage location unless the program specifies a transfer or other special instruction.

Control Unit (CU)

The control unit is a major component of the processor and is *responsible for the coordination and control of the activities within the computer*. It sends commands and control information to all the other components of the computer and in turn, the control unit receives results from these other components (feedback) outlining whether the commands were carried out well or not. The control unit always awaits the feedback for it to perform the next instruction. During program execution, the control unit reads the program instructions from the main memory and decodes them so as to know their meaning and then activate the other chips, which are to perform the tasks as per instructions. E.g. If the program statement requires that text be printed on paper, the printer will be activated and text will be sent to the printer to be printed out on paper. Therefore, the control unit is within the processor, and is the circuitry that locates, analyses, and executes each instruction in the program. Often called the Input/Output control unit or I/O controller.

Conversational Mode

A data transmission method in which there is an interactive dialogue between the computer and the user and implies a question and answer type of session.

Converter

A device that changes the representation of data from one set of codes, modes, sequences or frequencies to a different set, e.g. from binary to decimal or from cards to tape.

Core Storage

A *core is a small ring of iron*. A wire passed through the core and current was passed through this core in such a way that the core was magnetized, either *north* or *south*. For example, to represent data a core magnetized to be North Pole or South Pole would be holding a one (1) or a (0) respectively. An extra wire was made to go through the core. This wire was meant to sense the magnetism of the core and read the stored values from the core. Since core storage is non-volatile memory, it holds contents without power and is still widely used in specialized applications in the military and space vehicles. Thus, core storage refers to the type of memory that was used in computers in the early days of computing. A computer's main memory used to be called core.

Crapware

Crapware, sometimes referred to as *bloatware* and *junkware*, is software that is pre-installed on OEM laptops and cellphones but offers no benefit because it is a trial version or has a short lifespan. In exchange for special negotiations with the publishers, computer makers frequently include this software, which frequently helps to lower the overall cost of the machine for the consumer.

Cryptocurrency

Digital money known as *cryptocurrency* uses cryptography to secure transactions and regulate the issuance of new currency. All bitcoin users can examine and verify transactions that have been made on a distributed ledger, typically a blockchain. Since the cryptocurrency system is decentralized, no centralized authority, such as a government or bank, is necessary to oversee, manage, or create the money.

Cursor

The *pointer on the Cathode Ray Tube (CRT) screen that indicates the current position on the screen of the CRT terminal.* The underline character is the visual image on the CRT screen of the cursor's position.

Cycle Stealing

The system whereby execution of a program in the ALU is *delayed* for several memory cycles so that communication can take place between the input/output control and memory. After the communication is completed the program in the ALU continues as though nothing had happened. In this way, processing and peripheral operations can be performed concurrently or with some degree of overlap.

Cycle Time

The time required to access a single character of data from the computer's memory and make it available to the ALU or I/O controller.

Data

Technically, raw facts and figures, which are processed into information.

Data Accuracy

Data Accuracy describes records that are free of errors and can be relied upon as a source of information. Data Accuracy is the first and most important requirement of the data quality framework in data management. Data correctness is no longer "just" one of the qualities of the data. It is quite literally the most crucial factor in determining how useable and useful info is. By keeping data accurate and current, errors and inaccuracies that could result in poor decisions or privacy violations are avoided.

Database

A set of interrelated files that is created and managed by a database management system. A database is a sizable collection of digital information that has been indexed; it is sometimes referred to as a databank, a datastore, or simply as a DB. It can be searched, used as a reference, compared, edited, or otherwise modified with the fastest possible processing times.

A database programming language is used to create and maintain databases. Depending on the kind of database being used, there are various "flavors" of SQL, which is the most widely used database language. Each type of SQL has a different SQL syntax and is made to work with a certain kind of database. For instance, Oracle SQL, Oracle's version of SQL, and PL/SQL are both used in Oracle databases. T-SQL (Transact-SQL) is a language used by Microsoft databases.

A database-engine is a term used to describe a program that uses a database.

Database Administrator

An *individual* who is *responsible for the physical design and management* of the database and for the evaluation, selection and implementation of the database management system (DBMS).

Data Breach

A data breach is when sensitive information is accessed without authorization, frequently with the intention of stealing it and selling it on the dark web. These assaults have the potential to cause considerable monetary losses and reputational harm to a corporation.

Data Base Management System (DBMS)

Software that controls the organization, storage, retrieval, security and integrity of data in a database. It accepts requests for data from the application program and instructs the operating system to transfer the appropriate data.

Data Carving

When filesystem metadata is unavailable, *data carving*, commonly referred to as *file carving*, is a forensic technique used to reconstruct files from raw data fragments. It is a standard practice while performing data recovery, for example after a storage device failure. It could also be done as part of a debugging process on a core memory dump.

Data Center

The *department that houses the computer systems and related equipment.* The data library is under the data center, and the data entry and systems programming departments may also come under its jurisdiction.

Data Collision

A *collision* describes when one or more computers or networking devices attempt to send data at the same time to one computer, server, or other network devices. When a collision occurs, the computer, server, or network device sends a request to try sending the data again.

Network collisions can be determined on network hardware, including many network cards, by looking for an amber or red light illumination. Network collisions can also be detected using software or diagnostic programs on some network hardware.

Data Compression Protocol

Documents produced using computers contain data that is redundant from the point of view of the machine. Scientists have developed methods to remove redundant data elements so that the document is represented in as concise a format as possible. This is called *data compression*. The original document is not modified. The *two standards* that are predominant in this field are CCITT V.42 bis and MNP-5. Both *specify how data can be compressed when sending and decompressed upon reception*. The CCITT V.42 bis protocol allows a 4-to-1 compression ratio. Roughly speaking using a V.42 bis, one can compresses 400 pages of data into 100 pages before transmitting it over telephone lines. The MNP 5 allows a 2-to-1-compression ratio. Data compression requires *error control*; therefore modems that offer data compression always offer error control as well. In practice, a modem will offer all four error control and data compression protocols or it will offer none.

Data Minimizing

Data minimizing entails gathering and keeping only the information required to accomplish a certain goal. This improves privacy and lessens the possible effects of a compromise. Finding patterns and other important information from huge data sets is a technique known as data mining, commonly referred to as Knowledge Discovery in Data (KDD). The usage of data mining techniques has surged over the past two decades due to the development of data warehousing technologies and the rise of big data, helping businesses by converting their raw data into useful knowledge. Leaders still struggle with scalability and automation, despite the fact that technology to manage data at a large scale is always evolving. Through smart data analytics, data mining has improved corporate decision-making. These analyses' underlying data mining techniques can be classified into two categories: those that describe the target dataset or those that forecast results using machine learning algorithms. The most interesting information, including fraud detection, user habits, bottlenecks, and even security breaches, are surfaced using these approaches for organizing and filtering data.

Data Preparation Operator

The data preparation operators are members of the data processing department and are *responsible for data entry into the system, using key stations*. Normally, in the data entry section, each key station is manned by a data preparation operator who keys in data which is then stored in the buffer, ready for the central processor to validate it. If any of the data entered is invalid, the keyboard is locked and an error message is generated by the system. The keyboard will remain locked until the error is rectified or a tag is put on the error record to mark it for correction at another time. On the other hand, if the data entered is correct and valid, it is saved on magnetic disk, and the data preparation operator will then inform the data preparation supervisor of the same.

Data Processing

The capturing, processing of data to obtain meaningful and usable information, and the communication of this usable information.

Data Recovery

Network collisions can be determined on network hardware, including many network cards, by looking for an amber or red light illumination. Network collisions can also be detected using software or diagnostic programs on some network hardware. Data recovery is the process of restoring or retrieving digital information that is no longer accessible. Any file that was unintentionally deleted, misplaced, or damaged would serve as an illustration. Depending on the circumstances of the data loss, different processes are used to recover the lost data. In more dire circumstances, data recovery can entail retrieving information from a hard drive that was destroyed in a fire.

Debug

To *locate and correct an error in hardware or software.* Debugging software is finding the errors in the program logic. Debugging hardware is finding errors in the circuit design.

Any of the following may be referred to as debug:

Generally speaking, *debug* is the process of looking over and fixing mistakes in a program's source code. For instance, a developer may debug a program to identify the location in the code of a mistake so that it can be fixed or avoided.

The debug command in an FTP session can turn debugging on and off.

The Windows and MS-DOS command lines both support the debug command. For more information, please visit our debug command page.

Decimal

Meaning *ten* (10); the universal numbering system that uses 10 digits. Computers use the binary system because it is easier to design electronic systems that can maintain two states rather than 10.

Decision Table

A *list of decisions and their criteria.* It is designed in a matrix format that lists criteria (inputs) and the results (outputs) of all the possible combinations of these criteria. Decision tables are sometimes used in place of flowcharts for problem description and documentation.

Deck

A collection of punched cards.

Default

A standard setting or action taken by hardware or software if the user has not specified otherwise.

Demilitarized Zone (DMZ)

A *DMZ* is a section of a network that serves as a barrier between an internal network and the public Internet. It hosts services that are accessible to the general public while limiting accessibility to internal resources. An organization's internal local-area network is shielded from unauthorized traffic by a perimeter network known as a DMZ, or demilitarized zone.

A demilitarized zone network's major objective is to provide access to untrusted networks, such as the internet, while maintaining the security of the organization's LAN or private network. The Domain Name System (DNS), File Transfer Protocol (FTP), mail, proxy, Voice over Internet Protocol (VoIP), and web servers are just a few examples of servers that are commonly kept in the DMZ by organizations. To ensure that they can be accessible via the internet but not the internal LAN, these servers and resources are segregated and given restricted access to the LAN. A DMZ strategy makes it more challenging for hackers to acquire direct internet access to the data and internal systems of a company. A business can reduce the risks associated with its local area network, ensuring that employees can communicate effectively and share information with each other directly over a secure connection.

Businesses that have a customer-facing public website must allow internet access to their web server. By doing so, they would be seriously endangering their entire internal network. An organization might pay a hosting company to host its website or public servers on a firewall to prevent this, but this would have an impact on performance. Instead, the public servers are housed on a distinct and segregated network.

An organization's private network and the internet are separated by a DMZ network. A security gateway, like a firewall, that controls traffic between the DMZ and a LAN isolates the DMZ. Another security gateway that filters traffic entering from external networks guards the default DMZ server. Businesses that have a customer-facing public website must allow internet access to their web server. By doing so, they would be seriously endangering their entire internal network. An organization might pay a hosting company to host its website or public servers on a firewall to prevent this, but this would have an impact on performance. Instead, the public servers are housed on a distinct and segregated network.

An organization's private network and the internet are separated by a DMZ network. A security gateway, like a firewall, that controls traffic between the DMZ and a LAN isolates the DMZ. Another security gateway that filters traffic entering from external networks guards the default DMZ server.

Desktop Publishing (DTP)

Desktop publishing (or DTP) is the product of technological advances in personal computing, print graphics, and computer-generated typography. It *synthesizes the capabilities of typesetting, graphic design, book production, and plate making* in one integrated, cost effective hardware and software configuration. All of these functions are performed using the personal computer. DTP can be used to design and produce anything that can be printed: newspapers, books, posters, catalogs, journals, articles, or annual reports.

Desktop publishing allows the computer user to combine text and image files into a single document and then design a page that looks like a page in a book or journal. The text and images can be manipulated, that is their size and position can be changed as many times as necessary until the desired look is achieved. The operator can select different typefaces and type sizes, can format the text in several columns, or can run text around graphic images.

With a high-resolution computer monitor, the operator can then see exactly what the page will look like before the page is printed. What You See Is What You Get, or (WYSIWYG), has become one of the key advantages to desktop publishing. The page can then be sent to a laser printer for inexpensive page proofs or to a typesetting device for final printing. Desktop publishing software is becoming more sophisticated and accessible. Many programs allow for simple operations appropriate for newsletters, proposals, or announcements. Other programs allow for book-length formats and give the operator a high degree of control.

DTP can be combined with telecommunications technology so that newsletters, announcements, or other materials can be faxed to other sites for posting or distribution. Where mail service is inadequate, DTP files can be electronically transferred to remote computers so that those sites can print and duplicate documents.

An author, editor, or publisher can use DTP to convert manuscripts into final form without requiring the services of a commercial typesetter. You can store the text electronically, make corrections, and include revisions very easily and cheaply. New editions can be brought out frequently at little additional cost.

DTP can be used to organize the local production of textbooks and journals. Scientific communities can use DTP to publish and disseminate the results of their research. Above all, DTP offers opportunities for providing teaching materials that may have much more relevance for students because the material is selected by authors with local experience. They can draw on local information and use examples that may be more relevant than those in foreign texts.

Where the local market for a given textbook may only be several hundred copies in a given year and local currency availability may not allow prices to be high enough to cover costs, there may not be any incentive for local publishers to produce textbooks. In this case, universities and schools should consider producing their own texts with microcomputers in the relatively small numbers their classes might require. The currently available software permits almost all scientific formulae and technical drawings or graphs to be reproduced with a quality very similar to typesetting.

The skills required to operate this software at a professional level are not always easy to learn. The difficulties of obtaining good design, typography, and layout are not at all diminished by desktop publishing software. Indeed, one of the costs to consider when proposing a desktop publishing system is that of "creative time-wasting." Due to the flexibility of most systems, one can create virtually limitless designs and layouts for each and every page. It can also have the limitation that the author may receive neither recognition for the work nor royalties from the sale of it.

To use DTP, first, you need a basic personal computer. It is important to be able to see both graphics and text before printing, so a high-resolution monitor (computer screen) is very useful. A scanner can be useful if the text and images do not yet exist in electronic form. A mouse, or special input devise, makes manipulation of the text and graphics much easier. A laser printer is essential for printing the product. Desktop publishing application software for page layout is also needed. Packages that have been used in Africa include PageMaker and Ventura. New versions of personal computer software offer WYSIWIG so it is easier to see what you are doing with even basic word processing programs. Also, Windows-based software offers opportunities to integrate text, graphics, and data so that quality publications can be created from simple word processing programs.

Destination File

A file designated to receive information that is output from a computer run.

Detail Flowchart

A diagram that illustrates the order of execution of individual program steps.

Dial-Up

A modem is used to establish a dial-up connection. The modem has to connect to an active phone line that is not in use in order to establish the dial-up connection. The modem picks up the phone and dials a number associated with another machine while establishing a connection. The PC may check email, access the Internet, and share files after the connection has been established.

Digit

A single character in a numbering system. In the decimal system, the digits are 0 through 9. In binary, the digits are 0 and 1.

Digital

Traditionally, the use of numbers and comes from digit, or figure. Today digital has become synonymous with computer.

Digital Computer

A computer that accepts and processes data that has been converted into binary numbers (discrete data). All common computers are digital. Contrast with Analog computer.

Digital Data

Information represented by a code consisting of a sequence of discrete elements.

Direct Access

Pertaining to a storage device 0r procedure in which access to a particular address is such that the time required to transfer a unit of information to or from the storage device is independent of the location or address, which is accessed. Thus the access time for each storage location is the same.

Direct Address

A method of file accessing and processing in where the transaction record's key (or some part of the key) represents the location of the corresponding master record.

Disaster Recovery Plan (DRP)

A disaster recovery plan (DRP) is a written, organized strategy that outlines how a company can quickly restart operations following an unanticipated occurrence. A business continuity plan (BCP) must include a DRP. It is used in relation to organizational components that are dependent on an effective information technology (IT) infrastructure. A DRP seeks to assist an organization in resolving data loss and recovering system functioning so that it can function even if it functions at a low level following an incident. A DRP focuses on re-establishing the functionality of IT systems, applications, and data following incidents. Cyberattacks, civil emergencies, criminal or military attacks, and natural disasters are all examples of catastrophic events that can result in data loss and business disruption. Disaster recovery (DR) refers to IT technologies and best practices that are intended to prevent or minimize these losses.

Many companies, especially small and medium-sized ones, forget to create a solid, workable disaster recovery strategy. Without one, they have limited defence against the effects of very disruptive occurrences. After a tragedy, more than 40% of small firms will not reopen, and of those that do, an additional 25% will collapse within the first year. Planning for disaster recovery can significantly lower these risks. Planning for disaster recovery requires conceptualizing, planning, deploying the right technology, and ongoing testing. Data backup maintenance is a crucial part of disaster recovery planning, however backup and recovery procedures by themselves do not make up an entire disaster recovery strategy. Making sure there is enough storage and computing power available for reliable failover and failback procedures is another aspect of disaster recovery. In order to minimize disruptions to production operations and end-user experiences, failover is the practice of offloading workloads to backup systems. Reverting to the original principal systems is known as failback.

An organization must specify its data recovery and protection policies as cybercrime and security breaches become more complex. Rapid incident response can minimize downtime as well as financial and reputational losses. DRPs give firms a clear path to recovery while also assisting them in meeting compliance standards.

Disk Pack

A removable hard disk module that contains several hard disk platters mounted on a central spindle. The disk pack can be for storage of serial or direct access files.

Display Adapter

A *device that makes the text and graphics visible on the monitor*. It usually takes the form of an enhancement board that snaps into one of the expansion slots inside the CPU. The display adapter and monitor work together to translate the applications and data into something the monitor can use and we can see.

Distributed Denial of Service

A denial of service (DoS) attack aims to overtax the resources of a target system, render it inoperable, and prevent people from accessing it. In a distributed denial of service (DDoS) attack, a large number of compromised computers or other devices are used in a coordinated assault on the target system. DDoS assaults are frequently combined with other online threats. These assaults may begin with a denial of service to distract security personnel and cause confusion while carrying out more covert actions to steal data or do other harm.

DNS Spyware

When a hacker uses Domain Name System (DNS) spoofing, traffic is sent to a phony or "spoofed" website by changing DNS records. Once on the fake website, the victim can enter private data that the hacker could exploit or sell. The hacker might also create a subpar website with offensive or inflammatory content to harm the reputation of a rival business. The user's perception that the website they are accessing is trustworthy is exploited by the attacker in a DNS spoofing attack. At least from the viewpoint of the visitor, this enables the attacker to commit crimes in the name of a trustworthy business. Make sure your DNS servers are kept up to date to avoid DNS spoofing. Attackers try to use DNS server flaws, yet the most recent software releases frequently have patches that close known flaws.

Dot Matrix Printers

"INFORMATION SYSTEMS UNRAVELED: EXPLORING THE CORE CONCEPTS"

A dot matrix printer is *a printer that forms images out of dots*. It has a head containing a series of pins or needles held up in form of a matrix. Some common dot matrix printers have print heads with a matrix of 9x9, 9x7, or 7x5 pins. To print a character, the pins that are required to form a character are pushed forward out of the matrix slightly and the pressed against the print ribbon, which also presses against the

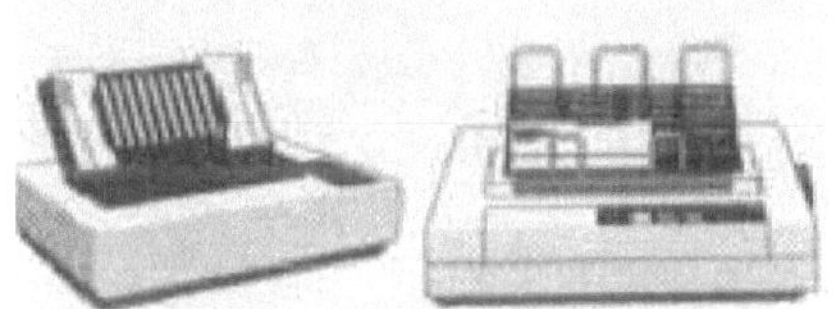

paper making an impact, hence the name *impact printer*. The more dot hammers used the higher the resolution of the printed image. The characters are represented as consisting of small dots, depending on the particular combination of pins for each character. There are two types of dot matrix printers, namely; *line printers* and *character printers*. These printers are relatively cheap and are being phased out, though they are still useful in applications such as printing of pay-slips, invoices and receipts, where a duplicate copy is required. Dot matrix printers use continuous multi-part stationery and interleaved with a carbon paper for production of duplicate documents.

Downtime

The time during which a computer is not functioning due to hardware or system software failure.

Drop

A connection made available for a terminal unit on a transmission line.

Dump

To copy the contents of all or part of a storage, usually from an internal storage into an external storage. See memory dump.

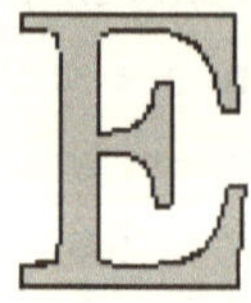

EBCDIC (Extended Binary Coded Decimal Interchange Code)

Pronounced "eb-suh-dick." Is a code developed by IBM that uses all of the 256 character combinations possible in an 8-bit structure.

Edit

To make a change to existing data. I.e. To insert or delete characters such as page numbers, or decimal points.

EDP

Abbreviation for Electronic Data Processing.

Electronics

The use of electricity in intelligence-bearing devices, such as radios, TVs, instruments, computers and telecommunications. Electricity that is used as raw power for heating, lighting and motors, is considered electrical, not electronics. Electronics deals with the motion, emission and behaviour of currents of free electrons, especially in vacuum, gas or phototubes and conductors or semiconductors. Contrasted with "electric" which pertains to the flow of large currents in wires only.

Electronic Commerce (e-Commerce)

The purchasing and selling of goods, services, or information over the internet and other electronic networks is referred to as electronic commerce, or e-commerce. It entails conducting business online, doing away with the requirement for a physical presence at physical sites. By providing a platform for online transactions, digital marketing, and electronic payments, e-commerce has transformed how businesses run and how customers shop.

Electronic mail (e-Mail)

The term "e-mail," which is short for "electronic mail," refers to data that is stored on a computer and sent between two users via telecommunications. E-mail, to put it simply, is a message that can include text, files, photos, or other attachments and is sent across a network to a specific person or group of people.

Ray Tomlinson sent the first email in 1971. Tomlinson sent the test email to himself with the subject line "something like QWERTYUIOP." However, even though he sent the email to only himself, it was still sent across the ARPANET.

Before the @ sign, the first component of every email address includes the user, group, or department of the organization. In the aforementioned illustration, "support" refers to Computer Hope's Technical Support division.

The "@" (at symbol) is a delimiter in the email address and has been necessary since Ray Tomlinson sent the first message for all SMTP addresses.

Finally, the domain name of the user's home is "computerhope.com". The TLD (top-level domain) for our domain is ".com". To direct email to the right destination server, the domain name is needed.

Emoji

Emojis, which stand for "*picture character*" in Japanese, are electronic pictographs that may be used to express messages. They were first popularized in Japan and are now used all over the world. Shigetaka Kurita created the first emojis, which gained popularity after being added to the iPhone in 2011.

Emojis can now be used in emails and text messages on iOS and Android devices because they are a part of the Unicode character set. They are regarded as one of the most rapidly expanding languages ever.

Users of computers or laptops running Microsoft Windows 10 and 11 can access a window that allows them to insert emoji, kaomoji, and symbols by pressing and holding the Windows key and then the period key.

Encryption

Encryption converts data into a format that is only understandable by parties with the proper authorization. This protects data while it is being stored and transmitted. The two main types of encryption are symmetric and asymmetric.

End User

Same as *User*. Any individual who interacts with a computer at an application level. Programmers, operators and other technical staff are not considered users when working in a professional capacity on the computer.

Endless Loop

A software section is continuously repeated in an endless loop, also referred to as an infinite or continuous loop. For instance, using the GOTO command to repeatedly refer back to the start of the loop can be used to construct an endless loop in batch files.

Error

An *error* is any unanticipated problem that prevents a computer from operating correctly. Either software or hardware mistakes can occur in computers. The amount of loss of precision in a quantity; the difference between an accurate and the calculated approximation. *Errors* occur in numerical methods; *mistakes* occur programming, coding, data transcription, and operating; *malfunctions* occur in computers and are due to physical limitations on the properties of materials.

Error Control Protocol (ECP)

Electrical disturbances (also known as line noise) corrupt data flowing through telephone lines. *Error control protocols help eliminate errors contributing to this noise and other glitches in the telephone system.* An error correcting modem will continually check to see if the data was received EXACTLY in the form it was originally sent out by the sending modem. This is achieved when the modem packs the data characters into blocks of data, and sends them; then the receiving modem checks for data integrity and asks for erroneous data blocks to be resent. The two common standards for error control protocols are the MNP-4 (MNP stands for Microcosm Networking Protocol) and the CCITT V.42 In order to work, both the sending and receiving modem must have error control capabilities that conform to the same protocol. In this regard, CCITT V.42 is preferable because it can "talk" to modems using the MNP-4 standard. In practice, most modems with an error control protocol include both standards.

Error Handling

Routines in a program that respond to errors. The measurement of quality in error handling is based on how the system informs the user of such conditions and what alternatives it provides for dealing with them. Poorly written programs may just hang up the computer when the wrong data is entered or a system error occurs, such as a disk error.

ERP

ERP, which stands for *enterprise resource planning*, is a *corporate system* that combines several software programs for accounting, human resources, inventory, orders, and shipping. Since they are frequently utilized by larger enterprises, ERP systems have been around since the early 1990s and fall under the category of enterprise applications. However, there are other simpler ERP software options for small businesses.

Error Rate

The ratio of the number of erroneous units of data to the total number of units of data transmitted. It is the measurement of the effectiveness of a communication channel.

Execution Time

The time at which an object program is executed.

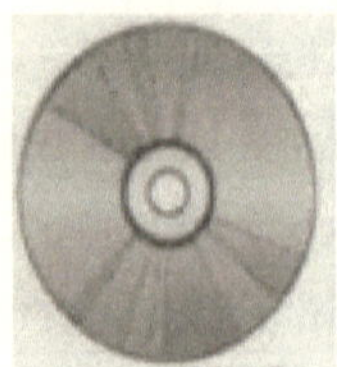 **External Storage**

External storage is also called *backing storage* or *auxiliary storage* and is peripheral storage that is outside the central processing unit (CPU), such as disks, CD-ROMs and magnetic tapes. The data and programs that are currently being worked on by the computer are kept in the main memory. The main memory is normally small as compared to the data and programs that is stored and retrieved from it. Therefore, the computer uses external storage devices to store data, programs, or information that is not being required presently in main memory but may be required at a later date.

Facsimile (FAX)

Originally called *tele copying*, it is the communication of a printed page between remote locations. Fax machines scan a paper form and convert its image into a code for transmission over a telephone system. The receiving machine reconverts the codes and prints a facsimile of the original. A fax machine is made up of a scanner, printer and fax modem.

Father-Son- Master File updating technique

A file updating technique that is characterized by the sequential access of both a master file and a transaction file. This technique results in a new updated master file and an old master file that is retained for backup purposes.

Fidonet

Fidonet is just one *form of electronic communications that provides a means to bridge time and distance to facilitate interpersonal communication.* The simplest and least expensive type of computer-based messaging is a bulletin board system.

In its basic form, the idea of a bulletin board is that any member of the system can post a message in a public area. Any other member of the system can browse through the bulletin board reading items of interest. Fidonet-compatible systems offer three main services: electronic mail (one to one communication), conference mail (many to many), and file transfers. *Fidonet file transfers can handle both text and binary files.* When these services are integrated with an interactive electronic bulletin board system such as Remote access(tm), they can be accessed by people using only a modem and ordinary dialer software. Simple bulletin board services and "Fido" networks are gaining in popularity around the world because of their low cost and ease of use.

Fidonet is known as the "people's network. In 1983, Tom Jennings, a computer programmer, began working on bulletin board software that would provide a link between the east and west coasts of the United States using homegrown bulletin boards. His scheme was loosely patterned after the amateur ham radio operators' network. A feature of the Fido software is that individual bulletin board operators can agree to a regular automated exchange of messages between their systems. This results in a web of linked Fido bulletin boards spanning countries and continents. This is collectively known as Fidonet. From its first appearance in 1984, use of Fidonet technology by the public has grown dramatically. Fidonet technology is gaining growing acceptance as an attractive computer-networking standard for educational, government, and business networks.

Fidonet technology encourages the creation of regional E-mail systems with a small host computer based in a developing country. Instead of using packet switching, these independent systems establish gateways with larger, international electronic mail systems using high-speed modems. At regular intervals, the independent systems dial into the larger systems to swap incoming and outgoing messages. In this way, members are able to communicate with users on other systems. This approach keeps down the cost of international calls without requiring sophisticated computer equipment.

Because Fidonet technology emerged in an environment where individuals operated each system independently and covered their own costs for phone calls and equipment, it had to be very flexible, decentralized, and designed to operate inexpensively with standard modems and microcomputers connected over ordinary phone lines. The "handshaking" and file transfer protocols built into all Fidonet-compatible software incorporate compression, error correction, and error recovery capabilities that squeeze as much data as possible into the shortest transmission time that the hardware will allow.

While the expansion of more advanced computer networking technologies is often constrained by prohibitively high costs and inadequate telecommunications infrastructure, Fidonet technology is not. It thus proves to be invaluable for people in countries where international dialing costs are high and line quality is often poor.

Fidonet-compatible systems, relative to other electronic mail and computer conferencing systems, are cheap and easy to install. They do not require powerful computer hardware and do not use packet switching and are thus attractive in countries that do not have highly developed computer and communication facilities. Gateways are now being developed from major international systems, such as Internet, to Fidonet nodes. The trend will be for the larger systems to offer comprehensive services, such as user directories and international database access, while the smaller, less formal systems will offer a forum for discussion among scientists and engineers.

Fidonet is a communications technology that many consider to be less advanced and, therefore, less useful than other technologies. It does not offer all of the sophistication that other, more costly systems do. Fidonet technology has a limit to expandability, insofar as it will always remain a store-and-forward, modem-based network. It lacks the capability for online information retrieval, database searches, remote-login, and remote-execution that other systems offer.

Basically, all electronic communication networks require the same minimal configuration. With Fidonet, the user needs a computer with a serial communication port, a modem, a communications software package and a phone line. With this set-up and some training, a user can participate in a variety of networking activities. The system needs the use of data access links (which may be a simple, ordinary telephone or an international packet-switched data network), a computer to act as "host" for the discussion, and a terminal device.

Fibre Optic

The science of transporting data, sound, and images by directing light through slender, transparent fibers is known as *fiber optics*, also spelt as *fiber optics*. Fiber optic technology is used to connect computers in local area networks and has essentially replaced copper wire in long-distance telephone lines in the telecommunications industry. The fiberscopes used for endoscopy, which is the examination of internal organs, and for visual inspection of the interiors of produced structural structures are also based on fiber optics.

A hair-thin fiber, occasionally composed of plastic but most frequently of glass, is the primary component of fiber optics. The diameter of a standard glass optical fiber is 125 micrometers (m), or 0.125 mm (0.005 inch). This is actually the cladding's or the outer reflecting layer's diameter. The diameter of the core, or inner transmitting cylinder, may be as small as 10 m. Total internal reflection allows light beams to travel through the fiber's core for significant lengths with very little attenuation, or loss of intensity. The light's wavelength and the fiber's composition both affect how much attenuation occurs over distance.

Field

A physical unit of data that is one or more bytes in size. A collection of fields make up a record, and a collection of records make up a file. Examples of fields are; name, address, sex, quantity, and amount due.

File

A collection of records; an organized collection of information directed towards some purpose. The records in a file may or may not be sequenced according to a key contained in each record.

Fileless Malware

Doesn't require the installation of software on the operating system is known as fileless malware. It enables native files, including PowerShell and WMI, to be altered to enable malicious functionality, making them harder to spot and recognized as legitimate.

File Maintenance

The periodic updating of master files. For example, adding and deleting employees and customers, making name and address changes and changing the prices in a product file. It is a periodic reorganization of a computer system's disks.

Firmware

A category of memory chips that hold their content without electrical power and include ROM, PROM, EPROM AND EEPROM technologies. Firmware becomes "hard software" when holding program code. It is loaded into the equipment at the time it is manufactured or later – by the person installing or using the equipment.

Firmware is information that specifies how a computer or other hardware device should function and is kept in the ROM (read-only memory) of those devices. Firmware, which persists on a device whether it is on or off, cannot be modified or removed by an end user without the use of special programs.

These devices' firmware can be updated using a software program known as a firmware update. A user might, for instance, download a firmware update that improves or resolves a problem with a network router. Hardware makers provide firmware updates. Sometimes firmware updates are made by computer enthusiast websites to provide a gadget even more capabilities than the maker intended.

These devices' firmware can be updated using a software program known as a firmware update. A user might, for instance, download a firmware update that improves or resolves a problem with a network router. Hardware makers provide firmware updates. Sometimes firmware updates are made by computer enthusiast websites to provide a gadget even more capabilities than the maker intended. Note that manufacturers frequently do not support upgrades from third parties.

Firewalls

A firewall is a piece of hardware or software that allows valid data to pass through while blocking suspect activity from entering or exiting a network. A firewall can be installed at a network's perimeter or utilized internally to create smaller subnetworks within a larger network.

Hackers are still cut off from the rest of the network if only one component of it is hacked. Firewalls come in a variety of styles and feature sets. Simple firewalls inspect traffic via packet filtering. Next-generation firewalls (NGFWs) that are more sophisticated include threat intelligence feeds, AI and machine learning, application awareness and control, and intrusion prevention as additional security measures. Firewalls filter network traffic in accordance with predetermined rules, obstructing harmful traffic and preventing unauthorized access. They are a fundamental form of defence and can be hardware or software based.

Fixed-Disk

A non-removable hard disk such as is found in most personal computers. Programs and data are copied to and from the fixed disk.

Fixed-Length Field

A field that contains the exact same number of bytes in each record. E.g. a 20-byte name field takes up 20 bytes no matter what size name is in it.

Fixed-Length Record

A data record that contains fixed length fields.

Flag

Any of the various types of indicators used for identification. Also a character that signals the occurrence of some condition, such as the end of a word.

Floppy Disk

A removable storage medium used with many computers many years ago. Also called a *diskette*, the medium itself is a single round disk of flexible, tape-like material that is housed in a square envelope or cartridge. The disk drive grabs the disk at its center and spins it inside its envelope. Can be recorded and erased hundreds of times.

Flowchart

A graphical representation of the sequence of operations in an information system or program, using symbols to represent the operation. Program flow charts shoe the sequence of instructions in single program or subroutine. Information systems flow charts show how data from source documents flows through the computer to the end-users. Different symbols are used to draw each type of flow chart.

Format

A Predetermined arrangement of characters, fields, lines, page numbers, punctuation marks, etc.

Formatting

Formatting is a process that is applied to soft-sectored disks before they can be used to store information. An un-formatted disk may not have the tracks and sectors that are needed for data to be stored on it. The process of formatting generates the tacks and sectors on a disk. In MS-DOS, the *FORMAT* command is used to accomplish this task. Formatting enables the computer to prepare the disk by electronically creating the tracks, sectors and allocating a *root directory* and *file allocation block* to the disk. When a disk has been formatted, the computer's operating system can now store and retrieve data from it with ease. The operating system cannot use an un-formatted disk since it cannot locate tracks and sectors.

FORTRAN (FORmula TRANslator)

The first high-level programming language and compiler, developed in 1954 by IBM. It was originally designed to express mathematical formulas, and although it is used occasionally for business applications, it is still the most widely used language for scientific, engineering and mathematical problems.

Fourth-Generation Computer (4GC)

"INFORMATION SYSTEMS UNRAVELED: EXPLORING THE CORE CONCEPTS"

A computer that is made up almost entirely of chips with limited amounts of discrete components. We are now in the fourth generation.

Fourth-Generation Language (4GL)

A computer language that is more advanced than traditional high-level programming languages. First generation languages are machine languages; second-generation languages are machine dependent assembly languages; and third-generation languages are high-level programming languages such as FORTRAN, COBOL, BASIC, Pascal, and C.

Fragmentation

The uneven distribution of data on a disk. A disk maintenance, or optimizer, program is used to reorder the files in a contiguous manner.

Freestanding Peripheral

Any peripheral device, which does not share with the processor portions of its internal logic circuits and power supply.

G

Garbage In Garbage Out (GIGO)

Refers to the fact that invalid input produces invalid output – what you get when you don't design a high-level of data entry validation into you application.

Gateway

A *device that connects two dissimilar LANs or that connects a LAN to a WAN*, a server, or a mainframe. It reformats the data so that it is acceptable for the new network before passing it on.

Gopher

Gopher; *the world's most widely used searching tool for the internet*, is a software program for browsing and information retrieval, developed at the University of Minnesota (whose sports teams are known as *"the Gophers"*). It provides a menu-driven interface that initially shows you what is available on one particular gopher server. The user burrows through a set of "nested" menus to get closer and closer to a specific topic. The advantage of Gopher is that it collects information that may be scattered across many computers in different forms and presents it on the same menu. If you select a menu item that involves making a connection to another computer, the connection is made automatically.

Graphical User Interface (GUI)

Applications, in which commands and other elements are represented by little pictures or symbols, often called *icons*. Many consider the pictures easier to understand and use than words.

GHz (Giga HertZ)

One billion cycles per second.

Any of the following may be referred to as GHz:

a. Abbreviated as GHz, the unit of measurement for EM (electromagnetic) wave frequencies equal to 1,000,000,000 (one billion) Hz (hertz) or AC (alternating current) wave frequencies.

b. A clock frequency, sometimes referred to as a clock rate or clock speed or clock, represents a cycle of time and is used to describe a computer processor or CPU. A crystal receives a modest quantity of power from an oscillator circuit that is measured in kHz, MHz, or GHz every second. The letter "Hz" stands for Hertz, whereas "k" stands for Kilo (thousand), "M" for Mega (million), and "G" for Giga (thousand million).

The first CPUs in computers ran at a frequency of kHz. For instance, the Intel 4004 was the first processor, and it ran at 740 kHz. Later CPUs ran at MHz rates; for instance, the Intel Pentium was offered in a range of frequencies from 60 to 300 MHz. The GHz range is where most modern processors run.

A processor can run and process data more quickly the higher its GHz value. AMD and Intel launched the first 1 GHz CPUs for personal computers in March 2000. Today's processors have several cores and operate at rates of 3.8 GHz or more.

GPS

GPS, which stands for *"Global Positioning System,"* is a system of satellites that assists users in locating themselves on Earth. After Sputnik was launched in 1957, the idea for GPS was born. On American Polaris submarines, the TRANSIT system went into operation in 1964 and enabled precise positioning updates. Later, in 1967, this was made accessible for commercial usage. The GARMIN nuvi 350, a GPS device used to discover locations while driving, is shown as an example in the picture. All 269 people on board Korean Airlines Flight 007, which was traveling from New York to Seoul, were killed when Soviet planes shot it down on September 1, 1983. President Ronald Regan instructs the U.S. military to make GPS available for public use as a result of this error.

Today, anyone can connect to these satellites and pinpoint their location to within 50 to 100 feet with the correct tools or software. Both cellphones and the infotainment systems seen in contemporary automobiles include GPS.

Grandfather, Father, Son

A method for sorting previous generations of master file data that is continuously updated. The *son* is the current file; the *father* is a copy of the file from the previous cycle; and the *grandfather* is a copy of the file from the cycle before that one.

Graphics

In computer terms, it is the creation and management of pictures. Pictures can be entered into the computer using input devices such as graphics tablets, mice or light pens, and existing pictures on paper can be scanned into the computer using scanners and cameras.

Grayware

Grayware, a phrase that was first used in September 2004 to describe unwanted software of any size that harms a computer system, is also known as greyware. The majority of spyware, malware, and adware programs fall under the grayware category. Generally speaking, *grayware* is less damaging than a virus and is more of an irritation.

Grayware can provide pop-up advertisements, lead to security holes in a network or computer, and possibly prevent users from carrying out specific tasks. Grayware can be removed with anti-spyware and anti-malware tools, which can also aid in avoiding new infestations.

GUI

To pronounce GUI, speak each letter individually (G-U-I or gee-you-eye). Sometimes, the word is pronounced "gooey." A system of visual, interactive components for computer software is known as a GUI (*graphical user interface*). A GUI presents information-conveying and action-representative items for the user to interact with. When the user interacts with the items, they alter their color, size, or visibility.

In 1981, Alan Kay, Douglas Engelbart, and a number of other researchers at Xerox PARC created the first version of the GUI. Later, on January 19, 1983, Apple released the Lisa computer, which had a GUI.

88

GUI items like as buttons, cursors, and icons are part of a GUI. Sometimes audio or visual effects like transparency and drop shadows are added to these graphic elements. Without knowing any commands, a user can operate the computer by using these items.

Hacker

In the 1960s, the term *"hacker"* was initially used to refer to a programmer or someone who altered computer code. Later, the phrase came to refer to someone with advanced knowledge of hardware, networking, programming, or computers, but without any ulterior motives. Ian Murphy, popularly referred to as "Captain Zap," was the first hacker to be found guilty of hacking in 1981. He entered the AT&T computer network, changed the internal clocks, and altered the billing rates system to bill consumers with lower evening prices during the day.

Hacktivism

"Hacktivism" is a mashup of the words "hack" and "activism." It discusses examples of hacking carried out to further or promote a political or other objective. Hacktivists can accomplish their objectives by using damaging cyberattacks like DDoS or by digitally vandalizing a website with a message or by eliminating content that disagrees with their opinions.

Half Duplex

Signals that move only one way at once, but in both directions. Half duplex, or HDX, in microcomputer communications is an online local echo that prompts a modem to relay a copy of transmitted data to the receiving computer screen.

Half Duplex Transmission

Only one direction of data transfer is possible during a half-duplex transmission. The majority of speakerphones only provide half-duplex, one-way communication. On the other hand, a phone is full-duplex and enables simultaneous conversation between both parties.

Handshaking

Exchange of predetermined signals for the purpose of control when a connection is established between two parties, like modems. When a computer connects to another computer or device, it performs a handshake. Verifying a connection, speed, or appropriate authorisation are stages that are involved. When a modem connects to another modem that is an instance of handshaking. The handshake, which is heard after the calling and shows that the computers are introducing themselves, is audible.

Hard Copy

A printed copy of machine output in a readable form, such as output from a printer. Contrast with *soft copy*, which is spoken or displayed on the screen.

Hard Disk

A magnetic disk made of metal and covered with a magnetic recording surface. Hard disks come in removable and fixed varieties that hold from 10 to hundreds of megabytes. Contrast with *floppy disk*.

A hard disk drive is a type of non-volatile data storage device (sometimes referred to as a hard drive, HD, or HDD). It is often installed inside in a computer and fastened directly to the motherboard's disk controller. It has one or more platters inside of an airtight container. Using a magnetic head that spins quickly across the platters, data is written to them.

A drive bay houses internal hard drives, which are connected to the motherboard by an ATA, SCSI, or SATA cable. They are powered through a link to the power supply unit (PSU) of the computer. The operating system, installed programs, and the user's private files are a few examples of the types of data kept on a computer's hard drive.

An operating system is necessary for a computer in order for users to interact with it and use it. The operating system analyzes mouse and keyboard inputs and enables the usage of applications like word processors, web browsers, and video games. A hard drive (or other storage device) is needed in order to install an operating system on a computer. The operating system is installed and stored on the storage medium, which is made available by the storage device.

The installation of any programs or other files you want to keep on your computer also needs a hard drive. Until they are transferred or uninstalled, downloaded files remain on your computer's hard disk or another storage media forever.

Earlier computers didn't have hard drives because they weren't developed yet or because they were too expensive. However, nowadays a hard disk or a storage device that serves as a hard drive is installed in practically all computers. Diskless workstations are the name given to the type of computer still in use today that lacks a hard drive and is frequently seen in offices.

A computer can start up and POST even without a hard drive. Other bootable devices in the boot sequence may also be checked for the required boot files, depending on how the BIOS is set up. You can use a bootable USB flash drive in a computer to start it up, for instance, if the USB device is specified in your BIOS boot sequence.

An SSD (*solid-state drive*) is frequently used in place of an HDD as the main storage component in contemporary computers. When reading and writing data, HDDs are slower than SSDs, but they have more storage for the money.

Although an HDD can still be placed as a secondary disk drive, it may still be used as a computer's main storage. For instance, the operating system and installed software might be located on the primary SSD, while documents, downloads, and media assets might be kept on the secondary HDD.

RAM (*memory*) and the disk drive may be confused by inexperienced computer users. RAM is a "volatile" data storage technology, meaning it can only store data when the computer is powered on, unlike an HDD or SSD.

Hardware

The mechanical, electronic and electrical devices or components of a computer, made up of system hardware and peripheral hardware.

a. ***System Hardware*** is the basic equipment, or components, needed to make the computer operate. The most basic computer system has four hardware parts. These are the computer itself, also called the central processing unit or CPU; the storage media or disks; the monitor or display terminal; and the input device, usually a keyboard or mouse.

a. ***Peripheral Hardware***, are the equipment pieces that are not essential to the basic operation of the computer but that may be necessary to perform certain applications. Peripheral hardware includes printers, scanners, and modems.

Hashing Algorithm

A hashing algorithm is an arithmetic procedure, which is used to change a key value into another value, which then serves as a storage address. Hashing algorithms are employed in computer systems so as to achieve direct access to records in files stored on direct access storage devices. Hashing algorithms can calculate a number in a fixed range from a larger key in a somewhat arbitrary manner. Thus, hashing involves deriving a storage address from a record key.

Hash Total

A method of ensuring the accuracy of processed data. It is a total of all the fields of data in a file, including fields not normally used calculations, such as an account number. At various stages in the processing, the hash total is recalculated and compared with the original. If any data has been lost or changed, the mismatch will signal an error.

Head

A device, which reads, records or erases information in a storage unit.

Hertz

The frequency of electrical vibrations (cycles) per second, abbreviated as Hz. (One Kilohertz = 1000 Hertz).

Hexadecimal (Hex).

Meaning *sixteen*; a base 16 numbering system used as shorthand for representing all the possible values in a byte. Each half byte (4 bits) is assigned a hex digit expressed in any one of the sixteen characters; 0, 1, 2, 3, 4, 5, 6, 7, 8, 9, a, b, c, d, e, f.

Hit Rate (file activity)

The *hit rate*, also called *file activity*, is a term used to describe the rate of processing of master files. The accesses records are referred to as the active records and therefore the hit rate gives a measure of how *active* the file is. E.g. form a file consisting 100 records, how many transactions are processed in a day? If say, Only 20 transactions are processed against a file consisting 100 records, then the hit rate is 20%. The formula to calculate the hit rate is thus:

No. Of active records x 100% = Hit rate

Total no. Of records in the file

Hollerith code

The code most commonly used to punch information into punched cards.

Honey Trap

Is when a social engineer poses as an attractive person online to communicate with a target. The social engineer creates a false online relationship and uses it to collect private information.

Housekeeping

A *set of instructions that are executed at the beginning of a program.* Housekeeping sets all counters and flags to their starting values and generally readies the program for execution.

Hybrid Topology

A *network topology* known as a *hybrid topology* employs two or more different network topologies. Bus topology, mesh topology, ring topology, star topology, and tree topology are some possible combinations of these topologies.

"INFORMATION SYSTEMS UNRAVELED: EXPLORING THE CORE CONCEPTS"

Whether a business, school, or user prefers a hybrid topology to a standard topology depends on those factors. The decision is affected by the quantity of machines, their location, and the desired network performance.

The following are the two types of hybrid topologies that are most frequently utilized.

- *Hybrid star-ring topology* - The star topology and ring topology are combined to form a star-ring hybrid topology. A ring topology links two or more star topologies collectively.
- *Hybrid Star-Bus topology* - A mixture of the star and bus topologies is known as a star-bus topology. A bus topology links two or more star topologies collectively.

PATRICK MUKOSHA

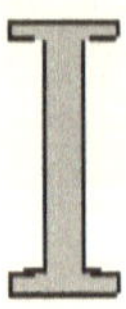

Icon

A *small, pictorial representation of an object, such as an application, file or disk drive, which is used in graphical user interfaces (GUIs).* The user selects an object by pointing to its icon and clicking the mouse button. Icons can be moved around on the screen.

iCloud

Photos, documents, and other media can be stored on Apple's cloud servers using the *iCloud* service. Then, users can access and move their files among iPhones, iPads, Mac PCs, and other devices.

Identifier

A symbol whose purpose is to identify, indicate, or name a body of data.

Identity

A group of distinctive identifiers or characteristics known as a "digital identity" can be used to represent a person, piece of software, machine, asset, or other resource in a computer system. Identity refers to the distinctive qualities and aspects that characterize a person or thing. Identity and Access Management (IAM) manages and authenticates identities to guarantee appropriate access.

A possible identifier is:

- Login information (username and password)
- Email address
- Number of a bank account
- IP address or MAC address
- Government-issued ID

To authenticate and allow access to resources, connect with other people, carry out transactions, and for other purposes, identities are utilized.

Incidence Response Plan (IRP)

A set of written instructions outlining the actions that ought to be taken during each stage of incident response is known as an incident response plan (IRP). Roles and responsibilities standards, communication strategies, and set reaction times should all be part of it. Organizations utilize an organized method called incident response to find and handle cybersecurity incidents. Preparation and prevention, detection and analysis, containment, eradication and recovery, and post-incident activities are the four steps of the NIST incident response framework. The National Institute of Standards and Technology (NIST) is a department of the US Department of Commerce that develops standards and guidelines for a variety of technological fields. The Information Technology Laboratory (ITL) at NIST is in charge of creating measurements and standards for IT, including information security. ITL created the Computer Security Incident Handling Guide (Special Publication 800-61), an influential paradigm for incident response (IR). The NIST incident response process is a cycle that incorporates continuing research and development to figure out how to secure the company the most effectively. Preparation, detection/analysis, containment/eradication, and recovery are its four primary phases. An incident response strategy Organizations may respond quickly and efficiently to data breaches, reducing harm and any legal liabilities, by having a well-defined incident response plan in place.

Indent

In structured programming, to indent is *to align text some number of spaces to the right of the left margin.*

Index

In data management, *a directory that contains the location of records and files on a disk.* Indexing is the most common method used for keeping track of data on a direct access storage device. An index of files contains an entry for each file name and its location. An index of records has an entry for each key field (account no., etc.) and its location. Indexes are maintained by the operating system or database management system.

Indexed sequential file organization and Access

A file is index sequentially organized if its records are sequentially organized and the file has an index, which can be used to locate the records in the file *directly*. The index is created by using a key field. Such an index forms an index file and is similar to the index found at the back of most student books. The index file contains the key field in the record and also a pointer that points directly to the location of the main record in the main file. This method speeds up access to records in the file. In other words, indexed sequential is a *method of file accessing and processing that uses sorted or unsorted transactions to update a sorted master file*. The method pairs each master file with a directory file called an index file; together these two files comprise an indexed sequential system. Each time a specific master record is requested from the master file, a search is made of the index file to reveal the location of the desired master record.

Indexing

A method of direct access file organization in which a part of the file is set aside as an index of addresses for information located in another part of the file.

The modification of an instruction by the contents of an index register in order to obtain a new effective address.

The use of an index register containing a quantity that is used under the direction of the control section of the computer hardware.

Index Register

A *high-speed memory circuit (register) that is used to hold the current, relative position of an item in a table (array)*. At execution time, the index register value is added to the instructions that reference it.

Informatics

It is useful to make a distinction between the terms information technology and informatics. *Information technology (IT)* means the group of technologies that is revolutionizing the handling of information. The term *informatics* is defined as *the study*, not of IT, but *of the consequences of Information Technology*, including the variety of ways in which information flows, is processed, is utilized, affects productivity and efficiency, is used for monitoring and control purposes, and, lastly, influences socio-economic development and society itself. This is analogous to the use of the term "economics," which refers to the study, not of the production and distribution processes and procedures themselves, but of how they are deployed to provide goods and services from scarce resources to meet human needs.

Information

A *meaningful collection of data*. Technically, data are raw facts and figures that are processed into information, such as summaries and totals. However, since information can also be raw data for the next job or person, the two terms cannot be precisely defined. Both terms are used synonymously and interchangeably.

Information Center (IC)

A *section within an organization's Information Systems (IS) department that provides personal computer tools, assistance and training to users*. IC personnel provide assistance with such software packages as query languages, report writers, spreadsheets, and financial planning systems. They are also available to provide ways of downloading data from the production databases in company's data center.

Information System

A *business application of the computer*. It is made up of the database, application programs, manual and machine procedures and encompasses the computer systems that do the processing. The database stores the subjects of the business (master files), and its activities (transaction files). The application programs provide the data entry, updating, query and report processing. The manual procedures document how data is obtained for input and how the system's output is distributed. Machine procedures instruct the computer how the batch processing activities, in which the output of one program is automatically fed into another program.

Infrastructure as a Service (IaaS)

The fundamental components of cloud computing, also known as IaaS or IaaS, include access to networking capabilities, machines (virtual or on dedicated hardware), and data storage space. With the most flexibility and management control over your IT resources, Infrastructure as a Service is most comparable to the current IT resources that many IT departments and developers are accustomed to today.

In-House

Any operation that takes place on the user's premises.

Initialize

To set counters, switches, and addresses to zero or other starting values at the beginning of, or at prescribed points in a computer routine.

Input

Any data ready for entry into the computer or to enter data into the computer.

Input/Output (I/O)

The transfer of data between the Central Processing Unit (CPU) and a peripheral device. Every transfer is an output from one device and an input into another device.

Input Devices

The *input device is the piece of equipment a user needs to tell the computer what to do*. The keyboard, which functions essentially like a typewriter, is the most common input device. Unlike a typewriter, however, the computer keyboard usually includes: a numeric keypad that works like a calculator; function keys that allow the user to execute special commands in different applications; and several special keys—alternative (alt), control, and cursor or arrow keys—that allow the user to make special keystrokes or move around on the monitor.

A *mouse* is a small device that augments a keyboard. It is a mechanical device with a ball protruding through a hole on the bottom. The ball's movements are tracked by sensors inside the mouse and conveyed through a thin wire (the mouse's tail) to the CPU and monitor. Newer mouse models have a motion ball that protrudes through the keyboard or through a self-contained unit called track balls. These devised allow the user to manipulate the motion ball with a thumb or fingers. Others are cordless. Many personal computers come with a mouse as standard equipment, and are activated by installing corresponding software called a mouse driver.

Therefore, input devices are peripheral devices that are connected to the computer through the input ports. They include mice, keyboards, scanner, joystick, joysticks, light pens, touch screens, scanners, optical character readers, voice recognition devices and digitizer tablet. Users, and other peripheral devices are able to transfer data and programs to the computer through these input devices, in a form understandable by the processor.

Input/Output (I/O) Ports

Input /output ports (interfaces) are ports to which peripheral devices can be connected. The computer and its environment (users included) are able to communicate through these peripheral devices, which include printers, video display units (VDUs), disk drives, keyboards and transducers; such as sensor in robotics.

Inquiry

A request for information from the storage.

Intelligent systems

Intelligent systems also known as *expert systems* are computer based systems that embody knowledge of the domain experts, offer intelligent advice or take intelligent decisions about a processing function using knowledge and interface procedures which otherwise require significant human expertise. An expert system consists of a *knowledge base*, an *inference engine, user interface* and *development engine*. The knowledge base contains the accumulated knowledge of the problem as rules, semantic networks, frames and logic. The inference engine provides the reasoning ability to interpret the contents of the knowledge base in a particular sequence. The user interface enables the user to interact with the expert system. The development engine is used by the domain expert with the help of knowledge engineer to create the expert system which essentially involves building the rule set.

For example, in the context of natural resource information, different types of information on multidisciplinary fields such as geology, soil, forestry, water, etc. are obtained from different media like topographic maps, aerial photographs and satellite imagery, etc. Interpretation and analysis of these information on natural resources is a complex process and relies heavily on human experts of various disciplines. The processing of these information using algorithmic methods does not provide satisfactory analysis and hence, a need for experts' system arises here. Every application in remote sensing deals with a specific field or a group of specific fields and therefore the expert's knowledge of those fields can be coded in the form of rules which will extract the knowledge from the database.

Intelligent Terminal

A terminal with built-in processing capability, but no local disk or tape storage. It may use a general-purpose CPU or may have specialized circuitry as part of a distributed intelligence system. Contrast with *dumb terminal*.

Interactive Session

A *question and answer type of dialogue* between the user and a computer.

Instruction

A statement in a programming language. Term associated with software operation.

Instruction Set

A computer's instruction set, often known as ISA (instruction set architecture), relates to programming, which is essentially machine language. The processor receives commands from the instruction set telling it what to do. Addressing modes, instructions, native data types, registers, memory architecture, interrupt and exception management, and external I/O make up the instruction set. The Intel 4004 was the first CPU, and it contained a 46-instruction instruction set. The instructions on modern computers number in the thousands.

The x86 instruction set, which is frequently seen on modern computers, is an example of an instruction set. While practically all computer processors employ the same set of instructions, their actual architecture might vary greatly. Both the AMD Athlon and Intel Pentium CPUs have almost the same x86 instruction set. A processor's hardware can include an instruction set, or it can be replicated in software by utilizing an interpreter. The simulated software version cannot compare to the efficiency and speed of the hardware design when running programs.

Instruction Cycle

The time in which a single instruction is fetched from memory, decoded and executed. The first half of the cycle transfers the instruction from memory to the instruction register and decodes it. The second half executes the instruction.

Instruction Register (IR)

An instruction register (IR) is *a high-speed memory circuit (register) that stores an instruction that is being executed.* Its results are transmitted to the control circuits, which generate the timing that control the various processing elements involved in executing the instruction.

Integer

A numerical literal that does not include any character position on the right side of the assumed decimal point.

Integrity

Integrity ensures that data are accurate and undamaged while being stored, processed, and transmitted. Integrity protection requires the use of systems to identify and stop illegal data alterations. Data integrity is preserved via methods like checksums, digital signatures, and version control.

Interface

A *connection and interaction between hardware, software and the user. Hardware interfaces* are the plugs, sockets and wires that carry electrical signals in a prescribed order. *Software interfaces* are the languages, codcs and messages that programs use to communicate with each other, such as between application program and operating system. *User interfaces* are the keyboards, mice, dialogues, command languages and menus used for communication between the user and the computer.

Internet

The Internet is a cooperative computer network of networks those links governments, schools, libraries, corporations, individuals, and others to each other and to vast information resources. The Internet protocol links many disparate and independent networks together so that they appear as a single network to the user.

You can use the Internet to:

- **Send and receive electronic mail messages**. At many institutions, special gateways permit staff to send and receive Internet messages via their regular PC-based e-mail system.

Email messages can be between individual users or among newsgroups, which are ongoing group discussions on many different topics.

- **Contact and search other computers** at remote sites (in Zambia, Europe, Australia, America, it doesn't matter where). This capability is called *Telnet*. Once a connection is established with a remote computer, you can search that computer as if you were sitting at a hard-wired terminal.
- **Copy files between computers**. This is called *File Transfer Protocol* (FTP). You can copy a file from your PC (or terminal) to a computer at a remote site, or copy a file from that computer to your PC. Many systems are set up with a special account that allows you to log in as "anonymous," using your Internet e-mail address as the password. This capability is known as "*Anonymous FTP.*"

The Internet works through packet switching. In 1964, researcher Paul Baran designed a computer communications network that had no hub, no central switching, and no governing authority. The basic technical idea behind his design was called packet switching. Each message is broken down into small pieces (packets) and put into a sort of electronic envelope with an address on the front. The individual pieces of the message are released into the network of interconnected computers and reassembled upon arriving at their destination. Packet switching allows for a fine-grained and efficient way of sharing expensive long- distance telecommunication circuits.

The Internet is an open network. Anyone or any group is welcome to use it, as long as that person or group has a terminal or a computer with the correct software and the ability to pay the costs. With the establishment of *internet-cafes*, users who do not have their own computers can have access to the Internet at a fee. In institutions, the computers used are attached to local area networks (LANs), which are, in turn, connected by a router (a device that connects networks together and passes information among them), to a regional or wide-area network.

A terminal can be used to connect to a computer (host) that is already attached to the Internet. This method is usually the least expensive but you must use the operating system of the host. You may also be limited in the applications you can use since the *Transmission Control Protocol/Internet Protocol* (TCP/IP) does not really come to your own computer; it stops at the host. For this type of connection, you will need a modem and access to a standard voice-grade telephone line.

Internet software can be installed in your computer and connect to an Internet router. This is more complex and more expensive. With a *Serial Line Internet Protocol* (SLIP) or *Point-to-Point Protocol* (PPP) connection, you can be a part-time Internet host. A SLIP/PPP connection allows you to use your own operating system and gives you direct access to a range of services. The TCP/IP suite resides on the local computer. A SLIP/PPP connection takes considerable onsite expertise to manage. SLIP software is available for IBM, DOS, Windows, Macintosh, and UNIX operating systems.

With a *leased line connection*, you can be a full-time Internet host. You will also pay a monthly charge for local connections. This type of connection provides the fastest service and you can, in turn, offer local resources and services to your user community but it also requires significant staff support and computing infrastructure.

No single organization owns or operates the Internet. Several thousand organizations administer their own individual networks and these combine to form the total Internet. This administration works because Internet is governed by a set of protocols that specify what each operator must do to format and route messages and manage the network elements.

The Internet Society is the international organization for global cooperation and coordination for the Internet and its technologies and applications. Created in June 1991, the Internet Society operates through an international Board of Trustees, its regional and local chapters, its secretariat, and several volunteer committees. These include the Internet Architecture Board, which approves standards and writes engineering rules, and the Internet Engineering Task Force, which discusses operational and technical problems.

The Internet has been likened to a "library without a catalogue." There is nothing that tells you what's out there, or where it is. There are no central directories of Internet information. Gopher, Archie, Veronica, Jughead, Wide Area Information Servers (WAIS), and the Worldwide Web (WWW) are tools supported by Internet that help the user to find and retrieve information.

Interrupt

A signal that gets the attention of the CPU and is usually generated when input or output is required.

Intrusion Detection and Prevention Systems (IDPS)

To check incoming traffic for security risks, an intrusion detection and prevention system (IDPS), also known as an intrusion prevention system (IPS), can be set up immediately behind a firewall. Intrusion detection systems (IDSs), which simply identified suspicious activity for evaluation, gave rise to these security solutions. Additionally, IDPSs have the capacity to instantly react to potential breaches by obstructing traffic or resetting the connection, for example. Denial of service (DoS) or distributed denial of service (DDoS) attacks, as well as brute force attacks, are particularly well-suited for detection and blocking by IDPSs. IDPS can take immediate action to stop or mitigate attacks by monitoring network traffic for indications of suspicious activity.

J

JPEG

JPEG, which stands for *Joint Photographic Experts Group*, is a digital image compression format and a common image type used with digital cameras and the Internet. To achieve more compression, the JPEG standard employs a lossy sacrifice. In the file extension used with IBM compatible computers, JPEG is also referred to as JPG. The picture is an illustration of a JPEG picture.

Jumpers

Jumpers give the computer the ability to shut down a circuit, allowing electricity to run on a circuit board and carry out a task. Jumpers are made up of tiny pins that can be concealed by a tiny plastic box (jumper block). When the computer is opened, the image shows pins 1-2 jumped for Normal mode and pins 2-3 for configuration mode. Computer peripherals, including the motherboard, hard drives, modems, sound cards, and other parts, can be manually configured using jumpers. For instance, a jumper can be set to enable or disable intrusion detection if your motherboard supports it.

Jumpers were used before plug and play to modify device resources, such as modifying the device's IRQ. Most users today don't need to modify jumpers on their expansion cards or motherboards. Jumpers are typically most likely to appear while installing a new drive, like a hard drive. ATA hard drives have jumpers with three sets of two pins, as seen in the image. The drive can be changed from primary drive, secondary drive, or cable select by moving a jumper between two pins.

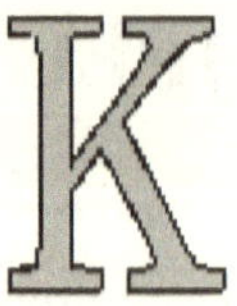

Key

1. The field by which records within a file are identified e.g. Account number, customer name, product code etc.
2. A button on the keyboard.
3. A numeric code that is used by an algorithm to create a code for encrypting data for security purposes.

Keystroke

A single key press on a keyboard is referred to as a keystroke. Every keystroke is a key hit. For programming reasons, keystrokes are utilized to react when a user presses a specific key. They are also utilized for keystroke logging, which records user keystrokes with or without the user's knowledge or agreement.

Typing tutor programs, which show users how to type more fast and precisely, are an example of software that records keystrokes. Keystrokes can be recorded by parental control software, giving parents access to what their kids are doing online. Businesses and educational institutions may also utilize keylogging-enabled software to monitor what their staff or pupils are doing online and ensure that there is no inappropriate or unlawful behaviour.

Kilohetz (kHz)

A kHz, often known as a *kilohertz*, is a unit of frequency equal to 1,000 Hertz. A measurement for wireless transmissions, audio signals, and alternating current are all done in kilohertz. A circuit's oscillator circuit, which is measured in kHz, MHz, or GHz, sends a little quantity of power to a crystal every second. The letter "Hz" stands for

Hertz, whereas "k" stands for Kilo (thousand), "M" for Mega (million), and "G" for Giga (thousand million).

The initial CPUs (central processing units) ran at kHz speeds. For instance, the Intel 4004 was the first processor, and it ran at 740 kHz. Later CPUs functioned in MHz; the Intel Pentium processor, for instance, was offered at speeds ranging from 60 MHz to 300 MHz. The speed of modern processors is GHz. A CPU can run more quickly the higher the speed (larger the number) is when measuring that speed.

MHz (megahertz) comes after kHz when determining the frequency (speed) of a CPU (central processing unit). Hz (Hertz) comes before kHz when determining the frequency (speed) of a CPU (central processing unit).

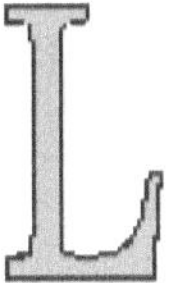

Label

In *programming*, a made-up name used to identify a variable or a subroutine.

In *computer operations*, a self-sticking form attached to the outside of a disk or tape in order to identify it.

In *data management*, a made-up name that is assigned to a file, field, or other data structure.

In *magnetic tape files*, a record used for identification at the beginning or end of the file.

In *spreadsheets*, descriptive text that is entered into a cell.

LAN (Local Area Network)

The need to communicate and share information gave rise to personal computer networks. *A LAN is the linkage of personal and other computers within a limited area by high- performance cables.* (A wide-area network, by contrast, is much larger and employs telephone lines or other long-distance communication media to link computers together.) LANs allow users to exchange information, share peripherals, and draw on the resources of massive secondary storage units, called file servers. *A file server is a high-performance personal computer that is not used exclusively by any individual on the network; rather, it exists to serve all the users of the network.* A print server is a personal computer that allows everyone on the network to use a certain printer.

LANs may simply link a few personal computers to a laser printer; more complex systems use central computers that enable users to communicate with each other via electronic mail, to share multi-users software, and to access shared databases.

Each computer linked to a network file server is also called a node or a workstation. The workstation runs application programs and serves as an access point to shared network resources.

Electronic *bridges* may interconnect individual LANs. A bridge is a device that enables two networks, even ones using different topology, wiring or communication protocols, to exchange data. A set of standards governs the flow of information within the network. These standards, or protocols, determine how and when a node may initiate a message. Network protocols also handle conflicts that occur when two nodes demand the same information or services at the same time. Common network protocols for personal computers are AppleTalk and Ethernet.

Network topologies fall into two groups: centralized and decentralized. In a centralized network, a central computer controls access to the network. This ensures data security and central management control over the network's content and activities. In a decentralized network, no central computer has control; rather, each workstation can access the network independently and establish its own connections with other workstations.

- **Bus Network:** This is a *decentralized network in which a single connecting line, the bus, is shared by a number of nodes, including workstations, shared peripherals, and file servers.* In this kind of network structure, a workstation sends a message to all other workstations. Each node in the network, however, has a unique address, and its reception circuitry constantly monitors the bus to determine whether a message is being sent to the node. All other nodes in the network, for example, ignore a message sent to a printer. The greatest advantage to this topology is that the failure of a single node does not disrupt the rest of the network. Another advantage is that it is easy to extend the network: you simply lengthen the bus and add nodes. The signal, however, cannot travel more than about 1,000 feet without an added device called a repeater. Most commercial LANs, such as AppleTalk and Ethernet, use a bus network.

- **Ring Network:** This is another *decentralized network in which a number of nodes are arranged around a closed loop cable.* It works like a bus network except that each node contains a repeater that amplifies and sends the signal along to the next node. Ring networks can thus extend far beyond the geographic limits of the bus network. One disadvantage is that the failure of a single node can disrupt the entire network.

- **Star Network:** This is a *centralized network with a physical layout that resembles a star.* At the center is a central node processor or wiring concentrator; the nodes are arranged around and connected directly to the central point. Wiring costs for this scheme are much higher because each workstation requires a cable that links the workstation directly to the central processor.

- **Token-Ring Network:** This is a *network architecture where all nodes are connected to the same circuitry, which takes the form of a continuous loop.* It combines token passing with a hybrid star/ring topology. A token is a special bit configuration that circulates continuously among the workstations and is read through a token-ring adapter card in each node as the token passes by. A node gains access to the network only if it can obtain a free token. The node that obtains the token retains control of the network until the message has been received and acknowledged. Token passing rules out the data collisions that happen when two devises begin transmitting at the same time, so it is a preferred topology for large networks with a high volume of traffic. Developed by IBM, this network uses a multi-station access unit at its hub. This unit is wired with twisted-pair cable (the cable used in telephone systems) in a star configuration with up to 255 workstation. The resulting network, however, is actually a decentralized ring network.

There are basically two methods for communicating information via the network's cables: *baseband* and *broadband*. A computer's signals can be conveyed over cables in two ways: *by analog* or *digital signals*. Analog signals are continuous ones that vary in a wave-like pattern. The number of variations or cycles per second is the signal's frequency, measured in hertz (Hz). Digital signals are discrete signals that alternate between high or low current. Because a computer's signals are digital, they must be transformed by a process called modulation before they can be conveyed over an analog-signal network. This is what a modem does.

Digital communication networks are called baseband networks. They use a communications method in which the information-bearing signal is placed directly on the cable in digital form without modulation. The advantage is that much less circuitry is required to convey the signal to and from the computer. In addition, many baseband networks use ordinary telephone cables and are, thus, much cheaper to install. They are, however, limited in geographical extent and provide only one channel of communication at a time. Most personal computer LANs arc bascband networks.

A *broadband network uses analog transmissions*. Because the microcomputer is a digital device, modems are required at either end of the transmission cable to convert the signal from digital to analog and back again. Broadband networks can cover greater distances than baseband networks and can convey multiple channels at one time. A broadband network can handle both voice and data communications.

The popular local area network standards, AppleTalk and Ethernet, are both baseband. AppleTalk can accommodate Macintosh and IBM-compatible computers. AppleTalk transmits at only 320 bits per second while Ethernet is capable of transmitting at speeds up to 20 million bits per second. AppleTalk's simplicity and low-cost make it an attractive option for modest size networks. It can link up to 32 nodes in a bus network. Ethernet, which was developed by the Xerox Corporation, can link up to 1,024 nodes in a bus network.

Thus, a LAN is a network of personal computers within a confined geographical area that is made up of servers and workstations. *File servers*, or network servers, are high-speed machines that hold programs and data shared all users in the network, while workstations act as user terminals. The *workstation* can be diskless, requiring all software and data to be obtained from the server, or it can have local disk storage for applications that are not shared by others. Small LANs can allow one computer to be both server and workstation, but the performance is improved when the server is an independent station in the network. Multiple servers can be installed for larger networks. Users may have their own printers or printers may be connected to servers and be shared. The controlling software in the LAN is the network operating software, such as *Novell Netware*.

LAWN

A LAWN, or *local area wireless network*, is a network that communicates with other computers or network devices via radio waves.

Laser (Light Amplification from Stimulated Emission of Radiation)

A device that generates a very uniform light that can be precisely focused. It is used in a wide variety of applications, such as communications, electro-photographic printing and optical disk storage. Lasers are used to transmit light pulses over optical fibers, which, unlike electrical wires, are not affected by nearby electrical interferences.

**Laser Printer**

A printer that uses the electro-photographic method used in a copier to print a page at a time. A laser is used to "paint" the dots of the light onto a photographic drum or belt. The toner is applied to the drum or belt and the transferred onto the paper.

Leased Line

A *telephone line or data line* that is rented from a phone company or data line provider by a private person or business. No unique number is necessary to connect to a leased line; it is always active. A T1 data connection is a fantastic illustration of a typical leased line.

Legacy

Any of the following examples of legacy:

Legacy refers to *antiquated* but still in use *software or hardware*. If a device is described as having "legacy hardware," it typically means that earlier hardware, like jumpers or dip switches, is used to configure it. For backward compatibility, a lot of computer programs and software may support or only partially support legacy programs and devices.

An electronic device operating outdated hardware and software is referred to as a *legacy system*. A legacy system would be one running MS-DOS from the 1980s, for instance.

Any *media that is seldom ever used* is referred to as legacy media. For instance, a floppy diskette is regarded as legacy media since alternative media, such as a CD and USB thumb drive, have taken its place and are now more often utilized.

When a superior option that offers more storage space, faster performance, and ease of use is introduced, media becomes outdated.

LIFO

Any of the following may be referred to as LIFO:

Also known as **LIFO** (*last in, first out*), this data processing technique sends the most recently received data out first. An illustration of how FIFO (first in, first out) and LIFO would operate is provided below. As you can see, the data is transmitted using LIFO in the same sequence as when it was last received. It is therefore inverted in this instance.

An essential data structure in computer science is the LIFO. The stack data structure is an illustration of the LIFO concept in action. A stack has no initial elements. A stack pointer is increased to point at the new "top" element whenever new elements are added or "pushed on" to the stack. The top element (located at the stack pointer index) is "popped off," i.e., removed from the structure, when elements are retrieved from the stack. In order to point at the new top element, the stack pointer is then decremented by 1.

Stacks are useful in many aspects of computer programming, including the evaluation of expressions, the parsing of syntax, recursive functions, and backtracking.

LIFO (*last in, first out*) is one way to manage inventory in a business. When a merchant uses LIFO, the item they purchase stays in their inventory until the item they already have in stock is sold. Because the cost of inflation on the existing inventory is not taken into account when using LIFO instead of FIFO to manage inventory, a corporation might claim a lower inventory value. Some nations have outlawed LIFO and mandated enterprises use FIFO due to the potential for misrepresenting an inventory's actual value for tax purposes.

Line Printer

A printer that prints one line at a time. Line printers are usually connected to mainframe or minicomputers.

Linear Programming

A mathematical technique that is used to obtain an optimum solution in resource allocation problems, such as production planning.

Line of Site (LOS)

Any of the following can be referred to as LOS:

Line of Sight (LoS) describes when a character or item cannot see another directly. Lacking LoS, which is frequently utilized in computer games, stops a player from taking actions like healing or injuring another player or NPC. For instance, common things that result in the loss of Line of Sight include walls, slopes, stairs, and trees. What elements of a game can interfere with line of sight is determined by the programming.

LOS, short for loss of signal, is a networking device indicator that indicates a signal or connection has lost or been terminated. LOS can happen for a variety of causes, such as the following.

- Network settings gone wrong.
- Help and support for networks and network cards.
- The actual device is subpar.
- There is a broken cable attached to the network device.
- On the other end, there is no connection at all.
- Relevant details

Liquid Crystal Display (LCD)

A type of monitor used in laptop computers. A *low-power display technology that uses rod-shaped crystal molecules that change their orientation when an electrical current flows through them.* LCD displays are flat and draw little power but they are not very bright.

Listing

Any printed output generated from a computer.

Log

A *record of computer activity* that is used for statistical purposes as well as backup and recovery.

Log-Off

To *quit,* or *sign off,* a computer system.

Log-On

To *gain access*, or *sign on*, to a computer system. If restricted, it requires users to identify themselves by entering an ID number and/or password.

Loop

In programming, a repetition of a function in the program. Whenever any process must be repeated, a loop is set up to handle it. A program has a main loop and a series of minor loops, which are nested within the main loop. Learning how to set up loops is what programming is all about.

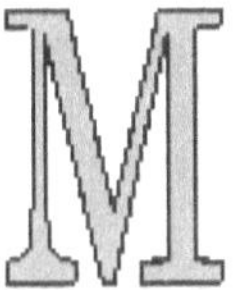

Machine Address: same as Absolute Address.

Machine Code: same as *Machine Language*.

Machine Cycle

The shortest interval in which an elementary operation can take place within the processor. It is made up of some number of clock cycles.

Machine-Independent

Programs that run in a variety of computers.

Machine Instructions

An instruction that the computer understands directly. It is made up of the operation code, or op code, and one or more operands. The op code specifies the type of instruction, such as INPUT. The operands specify the references to data or peripheral devices.

Machine Language

A language designed for interpretation and use by a computer system without translation. In order for a program to run, it must be in the machine language of the computer that is executing it. Although programmers may modify machine language in order to fix a running program, they do not create it. It is created by programs called *compilers*, *assemblers*, and *interpreters*.

Macro Instruction

An instruction in an assembly language program that refers to and is replaced with a series of instructions.

Magnetic Core: same as *core storage*.

Magnetic Disk

Direct access storage devices that are the primary storage medium for computers. Disks are analogous to phonograph records and turntables. The flat sides of the disk platter are the recording surfaces, the tone arm is the access arm, and the stylus (needle) is the read/write head. The major difference is that phonograph records are permanently recorded; whereas magnet

Magnetic Disk & Tape

The primary, reusable storage media for computers. Each disk or tape unit can hold from hundreds of thousands to hundreds of millions of bytes. When both media are available, the choice depends on the accessing requirements. *Tape is sequential; Disk is direct access.*

Magnetic Drum

A direct access storage device designed with a spinning cylinder like roll of paper towels. Its outside surface is divided into band-like tracks that run around the circumference. There are no access arms; a separate read/write head is fixed over each track. Drums used to provide the fastest retrieval, but are no longer widely used.

Magnetic Recording

The technique used to record digital data on disks and tapes. Writing (recording) is accomplished by passing the recording surface on or near a read/write head that discharges an electric impulse onto the surface at the appropriate time. *Recording* entails making magnetic polarized spots; representing a 0 or 1 bit, on the disk or tape surface. When tapes are recorded, an erase head clears the surface first, since blocks of data are not fixed in size as they are with disks. Reading is accomplished by passing the surface by the read/write head and sensing the polarity of the bit or changes of polarity.

Main Memory

The main memory is a device designed to store information (data, programs, intermediate and final results of processing) directly used in the course of performing operations in the computer's processor. The main memory is part of the Central Processing Unit (CPU) and works closely with the CPU during processing. Program instructions are transferred from the main memory to the processor where they are decoded so that the processor knows their meaning. Operands; on which program instructions operate to produce information, are also transferred from main memory. Thereafter, intermediate and final results of processing are transferred to the main memory for storage. Other external storage devices are also connected to the processor through the main memory.

Malware

Malicious software, or malware, is a broad term that includes Trojan horses, worms, viruses, and ransomware. Malware has the ability to tamper with data, stop activities, and take advantage of weaknesses. Also known as malicious software, malware includes spyware, Trojan horses, worms, ransomware, and viruses. These applications are made to hack into systems, steal information, stop activities, or demand money. Attackers utilize a variety of techniques, most frequently social engineering, to install malware on a user's device. Users could be prompted to perform an action, like opening an attachment or clicking a link. In other instances, malware installs itself without the user's knowledge or agreement by taking advantage of flaws in operating systems or browsers. Once malware has been installed, it can monitor user activity, relay sensitive information to the attacker, help the attacker breach other network targets, and even make the user's device a member of a botnet that the attacker uses for malevolent purposes.

Malvertising

Is internet advertising that is controlled by hackers and that, when a person clicks on the ad or even merely views it, infects their machine with dangerous code. Many reputable web publications have been found to include malicious advertising.

Man-in-the-Middle (MitM)

Users and devices assume they are in direct communication with the target system's server when they access a remote system through the internet. Attackers violate this presumption in a MitM attack by standing between the user and the target server. Once communications have been intercepted, the attacker may be able to steal sensitive information, compromise user credentials, and return various replies to the user.

Management Information System (MIS)

Information systems that have integrated the data for all the departments it serves. It implies a system that provides operations and management with the information they require. MIS was the buzzword of the 1970s, when online systems were being implemented within all large organizations. See *decision support systems*.

Manual Input

The entry of data by hand into a device at the time of processing.

Mark Sensing

Mark sensing is one of the systems used to input data into the computer system. Mark sensing systems utilize pre-printed forms or cards normally for selecting choices in appropriate boxes. The selection is made by marking the choice with a line or a cross using a pencil or pen. Marked forms are then fed into a reading device, which senses the boxes, which have a mark on them and then translate these readings into machine codes. These codes, in form of electrical signals, are the transmitted to the computer for evaluation. This system is called *mark sensing* because only the marks in the boxes are sensed.

Master File

A collection of records pertaining to one of the main subjects of an information system, such as customers, employees, products and vendors. Master files contain semi-permanent information which is usually updated periodically, such as name, address, as well as summary information such as amount due and year-to-date gross sales. *Contrast with transaction file*.

MashUp

The term mashup may refer to any of the following:

The term *mashup* may refer to an application or website that offers content from numerous sources and combines it in one place. This provides one location where a user can get information without having to visit several sites. An example of a mashup is combining news feeds from news sites (e.g., BBC, ABC and CNN) and making them all accessible on one page. This type of application or website is sometimes called an aggregator.

A **mashup** is an artful or meaningful combination of disparate elements to create a new, unique object. In music, a mashup may combine two or more songs from different artists or musical styles. The goal of an artist who "mashes up" different music is to identify similar themes or structures in unrelated music, and combine them in a pleasing way.

Math's Co-processor and Graphics Co-processor

Math's co-processors and graphics co-processors *are specialized and faster processors which work with the main processors on applications requiring high-speed mathematical or graphical computations, such as spreadsheet calculations or complex computer aided design (CAD) tasks.* The math co-processor supports the main processor by performing the required computations faster than the main processor itself. In a similar manner, graphics co-processors are designed to perform graphical functions, such as construction and maintenance of images much faster than the main processor. Though the co-processor improves the performance of the main processor, they are under the control of the main processor.

Memory

Memory is the computer's working storage that is physically a collection of RAM chips. It is an important resource of the computer, since it determines the size and number of programs that can be run at the same time, as well as the amount of data that can be processed instantly. Strangely enough, the computer's memory doesn't remember anything when the power is turned off. That's why you have to save your files before you quit your program. There are also memory chips that do hold their contents permanently (ROM, PROMs, EPROMs, etc.,); they're used for internal control purposes only and not for the user's data. The "remembering" memory in a computer system is its disks and tapes, and although they're called *memory devices*, many prefer to call them storage devices in order to differentiate them from internal memory.

Memory Address Register (MAR)

The memory address register is a memory chip that holds the address of the memory location from or to which data is being transferred.

Memory Chip

A chip that holds programs and data either temporarily or permanent. The major types of memory chips are ROMs and RAMs.

Memory Cycle

The time it takes to access a character in memory.

Memory Data Register (MDR)

The memory data register as well as the memory buffer register (MBR) is memory chips that contain the data to be stored into or retrieved from the addressed memory location.

Memory Dump

A *display or printout of the contents of a computer's memory*. When a program abends, a memory dump can be taken in order to examine the status of the program at the time of the crash. The programmer looks into the buffers to see which data items were being worked on when it failed. Counters, flags, switches in the program can also be inspected.

Memory Location

A space in memory where a unit of data can be stored or retrieved.

Memory Register

A register in storage of a computer, in contrast with a register in one of the other units of the computer.

Menu

A *list of available options and commands displayed on screen in an interactive program*. Selection of a menu option is accomplished by entering the number or letter assigned to it, by pressing the letter key of the first letter of the word or by highlighting the option and pressing the return key or the mouse button.

Menu-Driven

A program that is commanded by selecting options from a list.

Merge

To *produce a single sequence if items, ordered according to some rule, from two or more sequences previously ordered according to the same rule.* Merging does not change the items in size, structure, or total number.

Mesh Topology

A network configuration known as a mesh topology has devices such as computers and routers connected to one another. Most transmissions can be spread with this architecture even if one of the connections fails. It is a topology that wireless networks frequently employ. Here is a picture of a straightforward computer configuration on a mesh network.

Message

A *sequence of characters used to convey information of data.* In communication, messages are usually in an agreed format with a "heading", which controls the destiny of the message "text" which consists of the data being carried.

MICR (Magnetic Ink Character Recognition)

A *cheque encoding system employed by banks for the purpose of automating cheque handling.* Cheques are imprinted (using magnetic ink) with characters of a typeface and dimensions. MICR readers detect the encoded characters and convert them into digital data.

Micro-Segmentation

A network security approach called micro-segmentation allows security architects to logically partition the data centre into discrete security segments, right down to the level of each individual task, and then establish security policies and provide services for each segment separately. Instead of setting up numerous physical firewalls, IT may use network virtualization technologies to apply flexible security policies deep inside a data centre. Additionally, micro-segmentation can be utilized to implement application-level security controls that are policy-driven for each virtual machine (VM) in an enterprise network. Micro-segmentation software can dramatically increase a company's defines against attack since security controls are applied to distinct workloads. By applying the idea of network segmentation to specific workloads, micro-segmentation allows for fine-grained control over communication between various components.

Microprocessors

All personal computers are based on a special type of electronic circuit called the microprocessor. Often termed a "computer-on-a-chip", today's microprocessors are an elaborate arrangement of miniature transistors, called an integrated circuit or IC. *Integrated circuits are sometimes called chips because of their construction from a single piece of silicon.*

Microprocessors have built-in memory areas called *registers*. This is where they perform all their data manipulations and calculations. The signals going into the microprocessor are *digital pulses*, the patterns of which carry the command that tells microprocessor what to do. The entire repertory of these functions and their names is called the *command set*. The internal wiring of the microprocessor determines what it does in response to the command. In effect, a computer program, called *micro-code* is built into the hardware.

Microprocessors store and manipulate digital bits. They also move data around. The connections they use to move data in and out make up the microprocessor's *data bus*. To locate the data that is stored in memory outside of the chip itself, microprocessors use an *address bus* to indicate to the rest of the computer which memory area it needs to access. A *bus* is an internal pathway along which signals are sent from one part of the computer to another.

Microprocessors differ in the resources they devote to these functions and this affects the speed with which they will execute a command. Microprocessors can have different numbers of registers and the registers can be of different sizes. The number of bits they can work with at one time measures registers. For example, a 16-bit microprocessor has one or more registers that each hold 16 bits of data at a time.

The number of bits in the data bus influences how quickly the microprocessor can move information. The more bits a chip can use at one time, the faster it is. Microprocessors can have 8-, 16-, or 32-bit data buses. In addition, the number of bits available on the address bus controls how much memory a microprocessor can address. For example, a chip with 16 address lines can work with 64 kilobytes of addresses.

Each new generation of chip makes the microcomputer more powerful. The *first general-purpose microprocessor was the Intel 4004*, manufactured in 1971. Its registers handled four bits at a time. By 1978, Intel had introduced the 8086, a chip with a full 16-bit data bus structure. Intel introduced the 8088 a year later. This chip had 16-bit registers and 20 address lines. Its data bus, however, was 8 bits, allowing it to truly exploit the readily available 8- bit support hardware. IBM designed its first personal computer around the 8088 chip. Many computers in use in Africa today still use the 8088 chip, the first generation of computer chips for the personal computer. The *second generation* of computer chips came in 1984 with the 80286 (often referred to simply as the 286) Intel chip. This chip uses a full 16-bit data bus with 16-bit internal registers. It operates five times faster than the 8088. It also has superior memory; with 24 address lines it can address 16 megabytes of memory.

Intel's 80386 (often referred to simply as the 386) microprocessor is the first 32-bit processor to be used in personal computers. It manipulates up to 32 bits of data at one time and processes instructions two or three times faster than the 80286. The 80386's instruction set (the bit patterns it recognizes as commands to perform its various functions) is a superset of that of the 80286, so older software will run on the newer chip. But the 80386 has new features also. Protected mode includes instruction sets for managing memory, making it possible for an operating system to safely run several programs at the same time. Virtual 8086 mode, simulates not just one 8086 but an almost unlimited number of them, all at the same time. This mode thus allows a single 80386 microprocessor to divide its memory into many *virtual machines*, each one acting like it is an entirely separate computer equipped with an 8086 microprocessor. This means you can *simultaneously run* several DOS programs on one computer. This is called *multi-tasking*.

There are several types of 80386 microprocessors. Most are distinguished by the speed at which they run; speed is expressed in megahertz. The higher the megahertz number, the faster the processor. There are also DX and SX versions of the 80386. The DX communicates with RAM over a path that is 32 bits wide. The SX handles data internally, 32 bits at a time also, but it communicates with RAM at only 16 bits. The SX is easier and cheaper to incorporate into older PC designs.

Since the 80386 was released, Intel has also created an 80486. It too manipulates data 32 bits at a time but it includes two new features. One is a built-in 8 kilobyte RAM cache (see below) that works similarly to an external RAM cache to ensure

that the processor is not forced to wait for the data it needs to do its work. The other is a built-in *math co-processor*, a set of instructions streamlined for handling complex math.

The *Pentium* is the latest microprocessor from Intel. With more than three million transistors, it offers more processing speed than that of an 80486 DX. The gains are made possible by a new design that allows the microprocessor to carry out two commands simultaneously.

Mnemonic

Computer *instructions written in a meaningful notation*. An abbreviation that is easy to remember, e.g. CALCDIST for calculate distance.

Modem (MOdulator-DEModulater)

A device, which modulates and demodulates signals transmitted over communication facilities. A *modulator is included for transmission* and a *demodulator for reception*. Specialized modems are used to connect computers to a *broadband local area network*. The modem handles the dialing and answering of a call and controls the transmission speed.

Computers can communicate with each other over phone lines; that is, they can share and transfer data over the telephone. To do this, however, both the sending and receiving computers must have a *modem* (modulator/demodulator) that converts the computer information into audio signals. These signals then travel over conventional phone lines to a modem attached to another computer. This modem converts the audio signals back into information that the computer can recognize.

Modem can be either internal or external. An *internal modem* is an enhancement card that snaps into one of the slots inside the CPU. *External modems* are little boxes that attach to one of the ports on the CPU. Either kind of modem must be connected to computer and to a telephone line. The speed with which the modem transfers information is measured in bits per second (BPS); also called *baud rate*. Baud rates of 300, 1200, 2400, and 5600 are common on modems operating in Africa; although modems as fast as 9600 and 19,200 are available. The cost of high-speed modems is decreasing rapidly; this can mean big savings in transmission time. Where the line quality is poor or of variable quality, a high-speed modem will adjust to a slower speed to transmit the data.

To use a modem, a user must also have special communications software that, in effect, converts the computer into a telecommunications terminal.

Monochrome Display Adapter (MDA)

A *single-color display adapter* for IBM computers, and compatibles, that displays text, but not graphics with a resolution of 720 pixels horizontally and 350 lines vertically. An example of an MDA is the Hercules Graphics Adapter.

Monitor

The *monitor is the screen*; the device that displays the words or images that the computer user is entering or manipulating. Also called, *Video Display Unit (VDU)*, the monitor works in conjunction with the display adapter, which is often an enhancement board. The adapter makes the input readable to a human. There are, however, three things to consider when buying a monitor: *resolution, color,* and *size.*

Resolution translates as clarity: the higher the resolution, the sharper and more detailed will be the display. High-resolution monitors are important whenever graphics will be used.

Color monitors have now become almost standard and many applications require color displays. Monochrome monitors display a single color; white, green or amber are popular, against a (usually) black screen. Monochrome monitors have better resolution than color and are sometimes favored when resolution is a vital consideration.

Screen size is the diagonal measure of the display; the bigger the monitor, the more data it can display at one time. A typical screen displays only about one-half of a page. Large monitors are very helpful when page layout (desktop publishing) is the primary application but their high cost may not justify their use for everyday applications.

A *monochrome monitor* is a video display on which one primary color is available, usually white, with one background color, usually black. A monochrome display adapter (MDA) is a single-color display adapter for IBM computers that displays text, but not graphics with a resolution of 720 pixels horizontally and 350 lines vertically. An example of an MDA is the Hercules Graphics Adapter. It works only with graphics software that includes drivers for its non-IBM display format. For example, software designed to work with CGA (explained below) does not display graphics on systems equipped with the Hercules cards UNLESS the software specifically includes a Hercules driver. Many shareware and lower prices graphics programs do not include the necessary driver and will not work. Hercules display adapters work with all programs that display monochrome text.

A *Color Graphics Adapter* (CGA), is a low to medium-resolution color graphic system for personal computers. It is a bit-mapped adapter that displays either four colors simultaneously with a resolution of 200 pixels horizontally and 320 lines vertically or ONE color with a resolution of 620 pixels horizontally and 200 lines vertically. CGA monitors were the first to appear for DOS-based computers. A monochrome composite is a type of video display that attaches to a CGA. It does not provide color, but some models support "color" in the form of shading.

A *Digital monitor* is a Cathode Ray Tube (CRT) display that accepts digital output from the display adapter and converts the digital signal to an analog one. The CRT is an electronic vacuum tube containing a screen on which information is displayed. *Most common monitors and all standard TV sets use CRTs*. Digital monitors cannot accept input unless it conforms to a standard such as MDA or CGA (see above) or enhanced graphics adapter (EGA). EGA is a medium-resolution color system for personal computers. It is a bit-mapped adapter for IBMs and compatibles that displays up to 16 colors simultaneously with a resolution of 640 pixels horizontally and 350 lines vertically. Digital monitors are fast and produce sharp images; however, they do not display continuously variable colors. They display in only two modes: on or off. This makes it difficult to see subtle distinctions in color.

A composite color monitor accepts a standard video analog signal that mixes RED, GREEN, and BLUE signals to produce the color image. It does not provide high resolution. An RGB (Red Green Blue) monitor accepts separate inputs for each color and produces a sharper image. Although the enhanced graphics display uses RGB techniques, the RGB monitor is the same as the CGA standard.

An *Analogue monitor* accepts a continuously varied video signal and thus displays a continuous range of colors. *VGAs (Video Graphics Arrays)* are analog. VGA monitors display as many as 256 colors simultaneously, with a resolution of 640 pixels horizontally and 480 lines vertically. VGA circuitry is compatible with all previous IBM display standards. VGA uses an analog signal that converts digital information into different voltage levels that vary the brightness of a pixel. The process requires less memory than *EGA* and is more versatile. *Super VGA* has a resolution of 800 pixels by 600 lines; even more advanced adapters have a resolution of 1,024 pixels by 768 lines. A multi-sync monitor is capable of adjusting to a range of input frequencies so that it can work with a variety of display adapters—the higher the frequency, the greater the on-screen resolution.

VGA monitors, unlike EGA ones, preserve the aspect ratio of on-screen-graphic images. The aspect ratio is the ratio of the horizontal dimension to the vertical dimension. Unless the correct width to height ratio is maintained, the image will appear distorted.

Motherboard

Alternatively called the *mb*, mainboard, *mboard, mobo, mobd,* backplane board, base board, main circuit board, planar board, system board, or a logic board on Apple computers. The *motherboard* is a printed circuit board and foundation of a computer that is the biggest board in a computer chassis. It allocates power and allows communication to and between the CPU (central processing unit), RAM (random-access memory), and all other computer hardware components.

A motherboard provides connectivity between the hardware components of a computer, like the processor (CPU), memory (RAM), hard drive, and video card. There are multiple types of motherboards, designed to fit different types and sizes of computers. Each type of motherboard is designed to work with specific types of processors and memory, so they don't work with every processor and type of memory.

However, hard drives are mostly universal and work with most motherboards, regardless of the type or brand. A computer motherboard is located inside the computer case and is where most of the parts and computer peripherals connect. With tower computers, the motherboard is on the left or right side of the tower and is the biggest circuit board.

Alternatively referred to as an Apple computer's logic board, backplane board, base board, main circuit board, planar board, system board, or mb. The largest board in a computer chassis, the motherboard is a printed circuit board that serves as the computer's base. It distributes electricity and permits communication with the RAM (random-access memory), CPU (central processing unit), and all other computer hardware components.

Connectivity between a computer's hardware parts, such as the CPU, RAM, hard drive, and visual card, is provided by the motherboard. There are numerous motherboard varieties that are made to fit various sizes and types of computers.

There are different types of motherboards, and because of this, not every CPU and memory type is compatible with every motherboard.

However, regardless of type or brand, most motherboards can accommodate hard drives, which are generally ubiquitous. The majority of the components and computer peripherals connect to a motherboard inside the computer chassis. The motherboard, which is the largest circuit board in tower computers, is located on either the left or right side of the tower.

Multiprocessing

The simultaneous processing with two or more processors in one computer, or two or more computers that are processing together. When two or more computers are used, they are tied together with a high-speed channel and share the general workload between them. In the event that one fails to operate, the other takes over.

Multiprogramming (Multitasking)

A *technique that permits more than one program to time-share machine components*. This technique permits the concurrent handling of numerous programs by one computer. Multitasking is controlled by the operating system, which loads the programs and manages them until finished.

Multi-Factor Authentication (MFA)

MFA adds an additional degree of protection by requesting several forms of identification from users before providing access. By logging into your online accounts, or "authenticating," you are demonstrating to the service that you are who you claim to be. Traditionally, a username and password have been used to accomplish that. Unfortunately, that's not the best course of action. Sometimes usernames are merely your email address, although usernames are frequently simple to find. People frequently choose simple passwords or use the same password across numerous websites since passwords might be difficult to remember.

Because of this, practically all online services—including Microsoft 365—banks, social media, retail sites, and others—have introduced features to make your accounts safer. Even if it goes by different names, like "Two-Step Verification" or "Multifactor Authentication," the best ones all work on the same principles. You need more than just the username and password to sign into the account for the first time on a new device or app (like a web browser). To demonstrate who you are, you require a second item, or second "factor." When you attempt to sign in, a method of verifying your identity is one of the authentication factors. For instance, a password is a type of factor because it is something you are aware of.

The following are the top three types of factors:

- Something you are aware of, like a password or a PIN you have learned.
- Something you own, such as a protected USB key or a smartphone.
- Like a fingerprint or face recognition, something about you.

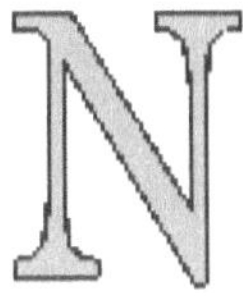

Nagware

Any software that prompts the user with a popup, notice, or window to complete a job or use a function is referred to as *nagware*. A nag message urging the user to register the software or buy a license, for instance, could appear when shareware or another program loads. Even more obnoxious nagware may show messages when the software is active at random times.

A checkbox or link that can be clicked in well-designed software allows users to disable or limit the appearance of *nag messages*. Some programs, however, may install software that enables them to run in the background and load each time the computer boots, displaying nag messages whenever they choose.

We advise deleting the program if nag notifications cannot be turned off or become too distracting.

Nanosecond

A billionth of a second. 1 second = 1,000,000,000 nanoseconds.

Netiquette

Short for "*network etiquette*". All forms of communication operate according to a set of norms and procedures. We tend to follow certain sets of manners when writing letters, using the telephone, AND in using networks for electronic mail. The rules established for network uses are called *Netiquette*.

Electronic mail is, by nature, an informal means of communication. Because e-mail messages are often written quickly and, once sent, cannot be erased or ignored, it is all the more important to follow some simple guidelines when using the networks for communication. The traffic sent out to the Internet may actually traverse several different networks before it reaches its destination. Therefore, users involved in this internetworking must be aware of the load placed on other participating networks.

"INFORMATION SYSTEMS UNRAVELED: EXPLORING THE CORE CONCEPTS"

As a user of the network, you may be allowed to access other networks (and/or the computer systems attached to those networks). Each network or system has its own set of policies and procedures. Actions, which are routinely allowed on one network/system, may be controlled, or even forbidden, on other networks. It is the user's responsibility to abide by the policies and procedures of these other networks/systems.

Unacceptable conduct, often determined by individual networks or discussion groups, can result in a temporary loss of network privileges. In general such conduct includes placing of unlawful information on a system, the use of abusive or otherwise objectionable language in either public or private messages, the sending of "chain letters" to lists or individuals, and any other types of use which would cause congestion of the networks or otherwise interfere with the work of others.

Netiquette rules include: -

- When using electronic mail, keep these rules in mind: Keep paragraphs and messages short and to the point. Focus on one subject per message.
- Be professional and careful what you say about others. E-mail is easily forwarded.
- Cite all quotes, references and sources.
- Do not use the academic networks for commercial or proprietary work.
- Include your signature at the bottom of E-mail messages. Your signature footer should include your name, position, affiliation and e-mail addresses and should not exceed more than 4 lines. Optional information could include your address and phone number.
- CAPITALIZE WORDS only to highlight a point or to distinguish a title or heading. Using all uppercase letters is like shouting. *Asterisks* surrounding a word also can be used to

make a stronger point.

- Use discretion when forwarding mail to group addresses or distribution lists. It's preferable to reference the source of a document and provide instructions on how to obtain a copy.
- Do not forward personal email to mailing lists or Usenet without the original author's permission.
- Be careful when using sarcasm and humor. Without face to face communications your joke may be viewed as criticism. (See smiley)
- Respect copyright and license agreements.
- When quoting another person, edit out whatever isn't directly applicable to your reply. Including the entire article will annoy those reading it.

Network

Individual computers linked in such a way that users can share software and hardware (for example, printers) and communicate with each other.

(See **LAN***)*

Network Administrator

An *individual who is responsible for the operation of a communications network.* The network administrator installs applications on the servers, monitors network activity and is generally responsible for its efficient operation.

Network architecture

The *design of a communications system,* which includes the hardware, software, access methods and protocol used. It also defines the method of control, e.g., whether computers can act independently or whether they are controlled by other computers that are constantly monitoring the network.

The *access method in a local area network*, such as Ethernet, Token Ring, and Local Talk.

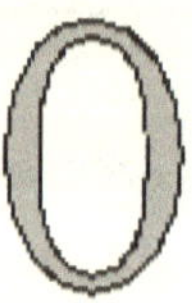

OCR (Optical Character Recognition)

Optical character recognition is one of the methods used to input data into the computer. This method *utilizes pre-printed forms or cards*. The user types in characters in particular positions on the card or form. The characters need to be in a particular font. The forms are then fed into the computer through the OCR reader, which translates the details into machine codes for the computer to process or storage. This system reduces human involvement in the process of data preparation and input. OCR documents are also examples of turn-around documents. Therefore, OCR is the *machine recognition of printed characters*. OCR systems can recognize many different kinds of special OCR fonts, as well as typewriter and computer-printed characters. Advanced OCR systems can recognize hand printing.

Offline

Pertaining to the operation of input/output devices or auxiliary equipment not under direct control of the central processor.

On-boarding

The process of integrating new hires into the workplace, assisting them in becoming familiar with their working environment and business culture, and making them feel welcome is known as on-boarding. It is essential because it increases employee retention, enables new hires to become productive more quickly, and is especially necessary for interns and remote workers.

New users are given the credentials, responsibilities, and permissions required to access resources during on-boarding. Companies go through the on-boarding process to welcome and integrate new personnel into the workplace. According to this definition, the employee on-boarding process goes well beyond the first day of a new employee's employment and continues until the individual has completely acclimated to their role and team.

And this is the primary distinction between orientation and on-boarding. According to the definition of employee on-boarding, any action that enables new hires to comprehend how things operate in their new workplace, become familiar with the business culture, and experience a sense of belonging and worth within their team.

On the other hand, the initial stage of on-boarding is employee orientation. It's during this time that new hires pick up the fundamentals of their surroundings: for instance, they may become acquainted with the workplace and company policies, comprehend their new job responsibilities, and meet their co-workers.

Off-boarding

The process of "off-boarding" an employee is just as significant as on-boarding an employee, while maybe being neglected more frequently. Off-boarding is the procedure used to remove former employees from the organization. Regardless of whether an employee leaves voluntarily or involuntarily, off-boarding should take place, but the procedures you should follow may vary based on whether the individual is quitting, retiring, or being fired.

Off-boarding enables a business to amicably part ways with a former employee. The Off-boarding procedure need to foster the development of your business. Off-boarding can also shield your business against claims of unlawful pay continuance, lawsuits, and other issues that may occur when an employee leaves.

Effective off-boarding guarantees that users' accounts and rights are deleted when they no longer need access, preventing lingering security concerns. The transfer from one employee to the next is made easier by an off-boarding approach. Off-boarding will provide your business with knowledge on what to look for when recruiting new personnel or reorganizing its structure.

Online

A system, or peripheral equipment or device in a system, in which the operation of such equipment is under control of the central processing unit. Information reflecting current activity is introduced into the data processing as soon as it occurs.

Operand

A piece of data upon which an operation is performed. In the instruction, **add a to b**, A and B are the *operands* (nouns), and ADD is the *operation code* (verb).

Operating System

An operating system is a master control program that runs the computer regardless of the application programs that are being used. It is the first program loaded (copied) into the computer's memory after the computer is turned on. It acts as the interface between a computer system and the applications that the users run on the computer system.

The operating system, which must be activated before any other applications can be called up and used by the computer, does not work alone. It depends on the cooperation of other programs and on meshing smoothly with the **BIOS**; (the **Basic Input/Output System**). The BIOS is a set of programs in read-only memory (ROM) on IBM compatible computers that facilitate the transfer of data and control instructions between the computer and peripherals.

The most popular and readily available operating systems are: -

MS-DOS

Short for Microsoft Disk Operating System, DOS is perhaps the most common set of programs for controlling microcomputers. It has been adapted by IBM for the personal computer family and runs on the Intel microprocessor series 8088 and later versions (see Technology Fact Sheet Number 12). Introduced in 1981, MS-DOS is marketed by IBM as PC DOS and the two systems are almost indistinguishable. MS-DOS is a command-line operating system with an interface that requires one to memorize a limited number of commands, arguments, and syntax. Once these basic commands are mastered, however, the user has a high degree of control over the operating system's capabilities.

The most severe limitation of MS-DOS is the 640-Kilobyte (K) RAM barrier that the operating system imposes. At the time MS-DOS was created, personal computers could handle only one megabyte of RAM, of which MS-DOS was able to access only 640K. Special memory- addressing schemes were introduced to expand or extend the memory. Intel's 80286 or later processors can only use extended memory. Extended memory is RAM above one megabyte that usually is installed directly on the motherboard of 80286 and later computers and is all directly accessible to the microprocessor. Under MS-DOS, expanded or extended memory cannot be used to hold program code; it can only be used to hold data.

b) **Windows 3.1**

The currently popular version of Microsoft Windows is not a true operating system because it requires MS-DOS; it cannot run a computer by itself. It extends the abilities of MS- DOS, however, and is thus described here. Windows recognizes the popularity of application program interfaces (API) such as those used by the Macintosh System. API allows one to use the same actions and interface procedures for common tasks such as selecting and deleting text, using menus, opening and closing applications, and printing. Windows is an optional API for MS-DOS and it solves many of MS-DOS's problems. It breaks the 640K RAM barrier, enables one to run more than one program at a time, provides an easy-to-use graphical user interface, and greatly simplifies program installation and configuration. Millions of older IBM PCs and compatibles exist that are NOT capable of running Windows. A minimal Windows platform includes an 80386SX running at 16 megahertz (but preferably at 20 or 25 MHz), at least 4 megabytes of RAM, an 80 megabyte hard disk, a 16-bit VGA video adapter and VGA monitor, and an inkjet or laser printer. Even better would be an 80486DX/33, with 8 megabytes of RAM, and a 200-megabyte hard drive.

c) (**Windows 95, 98 2000, millennium) and Windows NT**

This is a 32-bit version of Microsoft's Windows. It dispenses with DOS and provides better access to system memory than Windows 3.1. It allows programmers to use up to 4 gigabytes of RAM without employing extra or special technologies; it also offers enhanced fault tolerance, file handling, network access, and security. It requires 70 megabytes of hard disk space and 16 megabytes of free RAM. As such, it is beyond the capacity of most personal computers; it will find its niche in multi-user businesses and organizations that would otherwise use UNIX or OS/2 (see below).

d) **OS/2**

This is a multi-tasking (the execution of more than one program at a time) operating system that breaks the 640K RAM barrier, provides protection for programs running simultaneously, and enables the dynamic exchange of data between applications. Developed jointly by IBM and Microsoft, OS/2 has not done that well in the marketplace because of the introduction of Windows, which directly competes with OS/2's capabilities. Windows (with MS-DOS), which was supposed to be a stop-gap measure until OS/2 was accepted in the marketplace, has instead developed into the operating system of choice for many. IBM, in reply to Microsoft's moves, now has control of OS/2 development and it has recently announced a radical upgrade: OS/2, Version 2.1.

e) **UNIX**

This is an operating system for a wide variety of computers, from mainframes to personal computers. It supports multi-tasking and is suited to multi-user environments. UNIX is written in the highly portable programming language C and, like C, was developed at AT&T Bell Laboratories in the 1970s. UNIX is not easy to learn and use. Because AT&T was prohibited from marketing UNIX by the antitrust regulations then governing AT&T, UNIX was first provided without charge to colleges and universities. Different groups made various enhancements and, as a result, many alternative and mutually incompatible versions of the system are in use. Now, a standard UNIX is clearly emerging as AT&T has gained the right to market the system. Their System V version of UNIX, released in 1983, establishes a set of UNIX standards called the System V Interface Definition (SVID). IBM has adopted this standard for its own version of UNIX.

f) **System and System 7**

These are the operating systems for Apple Macintosh computers. They maintain Macintosh's technological lead in graphical user interfaces. System 7, released in 1991, is a state- of-the-art operating system that provides true multi-tasking, program launching from the menus, true virtual memory, and peer-to-peer file sharing on networked Macs without the need of a file server. (A peer-to-peer network is a LAN without a central file server and in which all the computers in the network have access to the public files of all the other workstations.) System 7 requires 2 megabytes of RAM but 4 megabytes is recommended if the user is to get the full benefit of its advanced features.

Operation

An operation is a program step undertaken or executed by a computer, e.g., comparison, multiplication, addition, data movement. It is usually specified by the operator part of an instruction.

Operation Code

The symbols that designate a basic computer operation to be performed.

Operator

The person who actually operates the computer and performs such activities as switching **ON** the computer, commanding the computer operating system, mounting disks and tapes (places input devices, removes output), and placing paper in the computer.

Optical Disk

A *disk that is written and read by light*. CDs, CD-ROMs and Videodisks are optical disks that are recorded at the time of manufacture and cannot be erased. WORM (Write Ones Read Many) disks are optical disks that recorded in the user's environment, but cannot be erased. Erasable optical disks function like magnetic disks and can be rewritten over and over again.

Optical Fiber

Optic fiber *is a very thin glass wire designed for the transmission of light*. Optical fibers have enormous transmission capacities capable of carrying billions of bits per second. Unlike electrical pulses, light pulses are not affected by interference caused by random radiation in the environment.

Optical Mouse

A *mouse that uses light to get its bearings*. It is rolled over a small desktop pad that contains a reflective grid. The mouse emits a light and senses its reflection as it is moved.

Optical Reader

An input device that recognizes typewritten or printed characters and barcodes and converts them into their corresponding digital codes.

Optical Scanner

An *input device that reads characters and images into the computer that are printed or painted on a paper form*. The scanner does not recognize the data its reading. Page recognition and image processing software do the actual recognition.

Output

Any *computer-generated information* displayed on screen, printed on paper, or in machine readable form such as tape or disk.

Output Devices

Output devices are *peripheral devices that are connected to the computer through the output ports*. Output devices include printers, plotters, display screen, cardpunch, and COM unit. They receive the results of processing from the processor and present them to users in a human sensible form.

Overlay

A *technique for bringing routines into memory from magnetic storage during processing, so that several routines will occupy the same storage locations at different times.* Overlay techniques are used when the total storage requirements for instructions exceed the available storage in memory. This process is inherent and automatic in a computer that has virtual memory.

Overflow Error

An *error that occurs when calculated data couldn't fit within the designated field.* The result field is usually left blank or filled with some special character in order to flag the error condition.

"INFORMATION SYSTEMS UNRAVELED: EXPLORING THE CORE CONCEPTS"

Packet

A "bundle" of data. In some types of electronic communications, data is broken into small chunks that traverse the networks independently. A group of binary digits including data and call control signals which is switched as a composite whole. The data, call control signals and possibly error control information are arranged in a specified format.

Packet Switching

A wide-area network that achieves high data transmission speeds by dividing information into 'sections' called packets. The packets are then transmitted by the most efficient route and reassembled at their destination. Thus, packet switching is a technique for handling high-volume traffic in a network by breaking apart messages into fixed length packets that are transmitted to their destination through the most expedient route. All packets in a single message may not travel the same route (dynamic-routing). The destination computer reassembles the packets into their proper sequence.

Page

A *segment of a program that is to be executed on a computer using the virtual memory concept.* Pages are stored on a direct access medium until they are called into the computer's memory for execution.

Page Break

In printing, *a code that marks the end of a page.* The user inserts a hard page-break, and the page will always break at that location. A soft-page-break is created by a word processing or report program based on current settings. Soft page breaks change as data is added or when the page length is changed.

Page-Line number

Six character which identify source statements to a compiler. The compiler sorts the statements by using the page-line number as a sort key. Also, called a *sequence number*.

Paper Tape

A *sequential access storage medium that holds data as patterns of punched holes*. It is a slow, low–capacity medium that, although extremely popular in the first half of the century, is in limited use today.

Paperless Office

An office in which all information is stored in electronic form......*Still somewhat a myth!*

Parallel Port

A parallel port is used to connect some peripheral devices; such as printers, to the computer. These devices receive signals from the computer in parallel. E.g., a character consisting of 16 data bits will not be sent bit after bit, instead the peripheral device will receive the whole 16 bits at once.

Parameter

A variable that is given a constant value for a specific purpose or process.

Parity

Parity is typically defined as having an even or odd quality. A parity check, commonly known as a VRC (Vertical Redundancy Check), is a data validation technique in computer science. When data is being transported or received from a storage medium, it is extremely helpful. The parity bit, a single piece of metadata that indicates whether the sum of the data bits is even or odd, forms the basis of the check. For instance, the computer would generate an error if a binary stream included an even number of "1s" but the parity bit was odd. Seven-bit binary values with an eighth parity bit are seen in the image.

Most memory manufacturers used to sell both parity and non-parity RAM chips in the past; parity RAM uses a ninth parity bit for every eight-bit byte. ECC RAM, which employs a more intricate kind of error checking, may be used in contemporary computers that need error-checking at the hardware level.

A *method used by most of the computer industry to determine whether hardware has correctly sent and received data characters*. If hardware checks for *even parity*, it considers valid all characters moved between units, memory registers, or memories whose total number of ON bits is even. If hardware checks for odd *parity*, it considers valid all characters moved between units, memory registers, or memories whose total number ON bit is odd.

Parity Bit

An extra bit attached to the byte, character or word used to detect errors in transmission.

Partition

A reserved part of disk or memory that is set-aside for some purpose.

Path

The logical course or line of direction taken by a computer in the execution of a routine.

PCMCIA

Personal Computer Memory Card International Association. Many notebook computers have a receptacle in the back that is designed to accept plugs conforming to PCMCIA standards. These slots can be used to plug-in peripherals such as modems or memory expansion cards.

PEER-TO-PEER Network

A Local Area Network (LAN) without a central file server and in which all the computers in the network have access to the public files of all the other workstations.

Peripheral

Any hardware device connected to a computer such as a monitor, plotter, printer, scanner, disk or tape drive, joystick and mouse.

Personal Computers (PCs)

Also called micros or microcomputers. Came into being in the early 1970s and are functionally similar to larger computers, though they serve only one user. Largely used at home and in the office for almost all applications traditionally performed on larger computers.

Microcomputers can be linked in a network consisting of mainframes, minis or just consisting of other microcomputers, by a modem. The micro's speed in based on the CPU that runs it, and its visual quality is based on the resolution of the VDU and printer. Their internal memory capacity can be up to the Megabyte range, while hard disk storage capacity is in Giga byte range. Usually, most micros include expansion slots to accommodate other peripherals.

PIN (Personal Identification Number)

A number chosen by the user as personal password for identification purposes.

Pin

One of the foot-like leads on the chip that plugs into a socket on the printed circuit. Is also one of the male leads on a multiple line plug, such as an RS-232 connector. Each pin is connected with its female counterpart to complete a circuit.

Pin-fed

A paper movement method that contains a set of pins on a platen or tractor. The pins engage the paper through perforated holes on the left and right borders.

Pipe

A pipe is a shared space that accepts the output of one program for input into another.

Pipeline Machines

Pipeline machines use the pipeline architecture in which each stage in the fetch-execute cycle is handled by a separate hardware unit. *Pipeline processing* is a technique in that provides simultaneous, or parallel, processing within the computer. Parallel processing refers to overlapping operations by moving data or operations into a conceptual pipe with all stages of the pipe operating simultaneously. E.g. while one instruction is being executed, the computer is decoding the next instruction.

Piracy

The illegal copying of software either for or commercial use.

Pixel

Short for *picture element*. The computer monitor is divided into rows and columns, forming hundreds of cells. Each cell is a single pixel: the smallest unit that can be manipulated by programmers and users

Pharming

An online fraud strategy in which a cybercriminal infects a server or computer with malicious malware. Users are deceived into giving personal information on a bogus website by the code, which automatically routes users there.

Phishing

Attackers transmit phony email correspondence that appears to be from reliable sources. The email may exhort the recipient to take an important step, click on a link to a malicious website, or download malicious software, prompting them to provide critical information to the attacker. Malware-infected email attachments can be found in phishing emails. ***Spear Phishing*** - is a type of phishing in which hackers target people with authority over security, like system administrators or senior executives.

Platen

The long, thin cylinder in a typewriter or printer that guides the paper through it and serves as a backstop for the printing mechanism to bang into.

Platform

The *hardware architecture of a particular model or family of computers*. The platform is a standard to which software developers adhere to when writing their programs, and may sometimes refer to the operating system included with the hardware.

Platter

One of the disks in a disk pack or hard disk drive. It resembles a phonograph record covered with magnetic tape, each platter provides a top and bottom recording surface. There are usually from two to eight platters in a hard disk and up to 24 in a large disk pack, with diameters ranging from 2 to 5 inches in small drives, and up to 15 inches in larger drives.

Platform as a Service (PaaS)

Platforms as a Service allow you to concentrate on the deployment and administration of your applications by removing the need for companies to manage the underlying infrastructure (often hardware and operating systems). As a result, you can run your application more efficiently as you won't have to deal about things like resource acquisition, capacity planning, software maintenance, patching, or any other undifferentiated heavy lifting.

Plotter

A Plotter is a graphics printer that draws images with ink pens. Plotters require data in vector graphics format, which makes up an image as a series of point-to-point lines. Plotters are still widely used in Computer Aided Design (CAD), and can produce quality drawings. *There are two types of Plotters*; the **drum plotter** and the **flatbed plotter**.

A drum plotter plots on a paper that is fixed to a drum. As the drum revolves back and forth, a bar suspended above the drum and containing a drawing pen moves from side to side and so plotting the drawing. In contrast, the paper on a flatbed plotter is stationary so that the pen moves up and down the paper, thus plotting the drawing. The drum plotter *uses continuous paper and can plot longer drawings,* while *the flatbed plotter can plot larger drawings.* Plotters can be operated on-line or Off-line.

Point of Sale (POS)

The system of data capture at the time and place of sale. Point of sale systems personal computers or specialized terminals that are combined with cash registers, optical scanners for reading product tags, and/or magnetic stripe readers for reading credit cards. POS systems may be on-line to a computer system credit checking and inventory updating, or they may be stand-alone machines that store the daily transactions until they can be delivered or transmitted to the main computer for processing.

Pointer

A pointer may be described as:

- A value in a register that points to an instruction or data.
- In database management, a pointer is an address embedded within the data that specifies the location of data in another record or file.
- In programming, a pointer is a valuable that is used as a reference to the current item in the table (array) or to some other object, such as the current row or column the cursor is on.
- A device such as a mouse that moves the cursor on the screen.

Polling

The technique used in multi-point service to determine when a terminal is ready to send data. The computer continuously interrogates all of its attached terminals on a rotating basis. If a terminal has data to send, it sends back an acknowledgement and the data transmission begins.

Port

An external connector on a computer that is used to hook up a modem, printer or other device. A port on a front-end processor connects to a communication line or modem. The port specified on a microcomputer, such as one parallel one serial port, refers only to the external connectors. However, the computer has several expansion slots that accept control units for devices, such as scanners, VDUs and disks. *To port* in programming terms is to convert software to run in a different computer environment.

Power down

To *power-down* or *shutdown* a computer is to turn off the computer in an orderly manner by making sure all application have been closed normally and the shutting the power.

Precision

The number of digits used to express the fractional part of a number. The more digits, the more precision. See *single precision* and *double precision*.

Pretexting

This is when a threat actor deceives the target in order to get confidential information. An actor who poses as a threat and claims to verify the target's identity may engage in a pretexting scam.

Preventive Maintenance

The routine checking of hardware that is performed by field engineers on a regularly scheduled basis.

Printer

A device capable of converting computer output into hard copy in the form of printed reports. The printer is probably the single most important peripheral device because it so integral to the operation of the computer.

The major considerations in buying printers are *quality, speed, noise*, and *adaptability*.

- *Quality or resolution* is measured as dots per inch (DPI). The higher the DPI, the better the quality. Printers with 600 DPI are about the norm. Lower quality printers can be used for printing drafts, citations from literature searches, and other non-essential documents. The higher the DPI, the more expensive the printer.

- *Speed* is measures in pages per minute (PPM) or characters per second (CPS). Speed may not be an issue if a high volume of printing is not expected.
- *Noise* is a consideration if the printer is being placed in a work area. Dot matrix printers are the noisiest; laser printers are very quiet. If you are asking your printer to do a lot, be sure it can handle labels, envelopes, or oversized papers.

Sharing printers often makes very good sense. Printers can be shared by wiring them to the computers via a switching box or print buffer or by connecting them to a network.

Dot-matrix printers are generally inexpensive workhorses that were popular in the early 1980s when personal computers first became affordable and readily available. They *are impact printers* that resemble a typewriter but the dot-matrix printer's use up to 24 metal pins and an inked ribbon. The pins receive instructions from the software application and can be combined in a variety of ways to print lines, curves, images, and characters. Dot matrix printers are noisy and their quality is lower than that of laser printers but they are reliable, efficient, and versatile. They use paper that is perforated along the side and is fed through the printer on tracks. A device called a *sheet feeder* that feeds one sheet of paper at a time can be attached. These printers are more compact than the laser printers.

Laser printers generate high-resolution output quietly and quickly. They print on single sheets of paper. The price of laser printers is tumbling but the operating costs remain higher than the dot-matrix printer does. Laser printers require expensive cartridges containing print toner; the laser equivalent of ink. Toner is hard to obtain in many African countries and must be imported at high-cost. Dust and humidity can affect the performance of laser printers.

Other printers include daisy wheels, ink jet, and thermal printers. *Ink-jet printers* are relatively low cost with high quality and are portable. *Thermal printers* require special paper that may be expensive and difficult to obtain in Africa. *Plotters;* which are used by architects and engineers, create elaborate and colorful floor-plans and illustrations.

Printer Buffer

A *memory buffer that accepts printer output from one or more computers and transmits it to the printer.* It enables the computer rid itself of its printer output at high speed and be used for another task while the printer is printing. Printer buffers with automatic switching are connected to two or more computers and accept their output on a first-come, first-served basis.

Printer Driver

A *software routine that converts an application program's printing request into the "language" the printer understands.* Modern printers require the user to install printer drivers before the printer can be used.

Print Queue

A location on the disk that holds output designated for the printer until the printer can receive it.

Print Server

A computer in a network that controls one or more printers. It stores the print image output from the users of the system and feeds it to the printer a job at a time. The printer server function can be added to a network server that provides other file sharing.

Print Spooler

A *computer program that facilitates printing to be done in the background while other tasks are being performed in the foreground.* For example, when a word processor or desktop publishing program is told to print, it generally creates a temporary file that contains text together with special codes for the printer. This takes a lot of processing time, but sending the resulting file to the printer doesn't. Thus this second step can often be overlapped with an interactive application without appreciably slowing it down.

Print to Disk

The system of *redirecting output to the disk instead of sending it to the printer* as is normally the case. The print image file that is created contains the text and all the required layout, or format, codes embedded within it. The file can then be printed at a later date or at a remote location by transmitting it to the printer without requiring the word processor or desktop publishing program that created it.

Printed Circuit Board

A flat board that holds chips and other electronic components. The back side of the board is "printed" with electrically conductive pathways between the components. The printed circuit boards of the 1960's connected discrete (elementary) components together. The printed circuit board of the 1990's connects microchips together, each chip containing hundreds of thousands of elementary components

Privileged Access Management (PAM)

PAM is concerned with protecting access for privileged users like administrators. To stop misuse, strong controls and oversight are implemented. By monitoring, spotting, and preventing unwanted privileged access to vital resources, *privileged access management* (PAM), an identity security solution, aids in defending enterprises from cyber threats. PAM gives you visibility into who is using privileged accounts and what they are doing while logged in by combining people, procedures, and technology. While extra layers of security reduce data breaches by threat actors, system security is increased by limiting the number of users who have access to administrative functions.

Process

To process is *to manipulate data in the computer.* The computer is deemed processing no matter what action is taken upon the data. In order to evaluate a computer system's performance, the time it takes to process data internally is analyzed separately from the time it takes to get data in and out of the computer. Input/output is usually more time consuming than processing.

Processor (same as **CPU**)

Program

A computer program is *a sequenced set of instructions to a computer to do a particular job*. A program is called *software*; hence, program, software and instructions are synonymous. A program is written in a programming language and is converted into the computer's machine language by software called assemblers and compilers. A computer program calls for data in an input-process-output sequence. After data has been input into the program's buffers from the peripheral device, such as a keyboard or disk, it is processed. The results are then output to the peripheral device such as a VDU or a printer. If data has been updated it is output back onto the disk.

Programmable

Programmable simply means *the capability of following instructions*. The computer's programmability is what distinguishes it from other electronic devices. Memory chips called Read Only Memory (ROM) are programmed by the manufacturer at the time of manufacture and data stored in ROMs can only be read and not changed. However, there are certain chips, which are programmable, such as the Programmable Read Only Memory (PROMs). A PROM is a ROM, which is programmed, not by the manufacturer but by the user and once programmed, the information stored on it cannot be changed. On the other hand, the Erasable Programmable Read Only Memory (EPROM) and Electrical Erasable PROM (EEPROM) can be erased electronically.

Program Counter (PC)

The program counter, also called *sequence control register* monitors the execution of a program. When the program is being executed, the contents of the program counter are updated to correspond to the address of the next instruction to be executed. Thus, the program counter points to the next instruction that is should be retrieved from memory.

Program Generator (*also called* **Application Generator**)

Software that generates application programs from descriptions of the problem other than from detailed programming. It is one or more level higher than a high-level language, but still require that the user enters mathematical, or algorithmic, expressions in order to describe complex functions. E.g. a complicated pricing routine in an order entry application would take a bit of programming to enter no matter how high-level the application generator.

Program Maintenance

The process of updating the programs to reflect changes in the organization's business or to adapt to new operating environments.

Programmer

An individual who designs the logic for and writes lines of codes of a computer program. Check *application programmer* and *systems programmer*.

Programmer/Analyst (*also called* **Analyst/Programmer**)

An individual who analyses and designs information systems and designs and writes application programs for the system. A programmer/analyst is both systems analyst and application programmer.

Programming

Programming *is the discipline of writing a sequence of instructions, called a "program", to control a computer.* Computer instructions are often called "statements". Some statements are called "declarations" or "definitions", because their main role is to specify information. Other statements are called "executable" statements, because they make the computer perform (execute) actions.

Therefore, programming is the actual creation of a computer program, using the following steps:

- Developing the program logic to solve a particular problem
- Writing the program logic in a specific programming language (coding the program).
- Assembling or compiling the program to turn it into machine language.
- Testing and debugging the program, and
- Preparing the necessary documentation. Proper documentation ensures easy program maintenance and continuity.
- Getting the program logic *(semantics)* is the most difficult part of programming.
- Learning the grammar *(syntax)* and writing the language statements *(coding)* is comparatively easy once the solution has been developed.

Prompt

A *message from the software that requests some action by the user*, such as "Press F1 for Help" or "Enter Customer Name" etc. It can also be a cryptic symbol that indicates it is ready to accept a command e.g., in MS-DOS a prompt is a right arrow "> ".

Protocol

In communications, a protocol is a *set of rules and regulations that govern the transmitting and receiving of data.*

Prototyping

The *creation of a system on a trial basis for testing and approval.* With regard to information systems development, prototyping has become essential for clarifying information requirements. Traditionally, the functional specifications, which are the blueprint and design of the information system, must be finalized and frozen before the system can be built. Whereas the analytically minded individual may have a clear picture of information requirements, the other people may not.

Public Key Infrastructure (PKI)

A public key and a private key are generated for an entity using public-key infrastructure (PKI), a data security technique. Blockchain networks utilize public-key cryptography to authenticate user identities and demonstrate ownership of digital assets. There are public and private keys associated with some decentralized IDs, such as an Ethereum account. The private keys can sign and decode communications for this account, while the public key identifies the account's controller. PKI uses cryptographic signatures (opens in a new tab) to validate all claims and offers the evidence required to authenticate entities, prohibit impersonation, and stop the use of false identities.

Pull-Down Menu (also called *Pop-up menu*)

This is a screen menu that is displayed on the screen from the top of the screen downward when its title is selected. The menu remains displayed while the mouse button is depressed. To select a menu item, the highlight bar is moved (with the mouse) to the appropriate line and the mouse button is let go. In contrast, a *drop-down menu* keeps the menu open after its title has been selected. A menu item is selected when the highlight bar is moved to the line and the mouse button is clicked.

Punched Card

This is a storage made of card stock that holds data as patterns of punched holes. A typical punched card has 80 or 96 columns, each of which contains 12 punching positions, capable of storing one character. The holes are punched into the card by a keypunch machine or card punch connected to a computer. A card reader reads cards into the computer.

"INFORMATION SYSTEMS UNRAVELED: EXPLORING THE CORE CONCEPTS"

Query

A question could be about any of the following:

a. The term "*query*" generally refers to a request or question made by a user, another computer, or a device. For instance, the text you type into a search engine (like Google) is known as the search query or search text, and each word is referred to as a keyword.

b. A *query* is a field or choice in a database or search that is used to find data in that database or somewhere else. For instance, you could use a database query to discover any associated tables that correspond to the American state of "Utah". The database may then produce a list of every Utah resident currently registered with it. A query is a system used to interrogate a database that allows a user to count, sum and list selected records contained in the database, using a query language.

Query Language

A generalized language that allows the user the flexibility of selecting records in so many ways from the database. Query languages provide either a command language, a menu-driven method or a query by example (QBE) format for expressing the matching condition. Query languages are usually included in the database management system (DBMS) and stand-alone packages are available for interrogating files that are part of non-DBMS applications.

Queue

A *queue* is a temporary area used to hold requests made when those requests can't be quickly fulfilled. For instance, a printer queue may occasionally receive print tasks from several users as well as from various programs. The queue management software handles incoming requests when the printer is occupied because it can only print one page of one document at a time.

Quit

To *exit the current computer program*. It is good practice to exit the computer program before turning the computer off as some programs do not close all files properly and may result in loss of some vital piece of information.

Quota

Disk quota management, often known as *quota management*, is a term for the administrator-granted permissions that place storage space restrictions on users, workgroups, and other groups. By establishing a quota, users can still save files while preventing a server or share from filling up with data.

Due to the over quota alerts, which are an indicator that users have used up all of their available space, most users who send and receive email or maintain websites may be familiar with limits. A similar message will also appear if an email attachment is too large to fit inside the allocated quota.

QWERTY

Christopher Sholes, who also went by the name "Sholes," created the QWERTY keyboard. On July 14, 1868, he was granted a patent for a typewriter. The official computer keyboard standard (ISO 9995) is the QWERTY keyboard, which takes its name from the first five alphabetic letter keys on the top row of keys. The QWERTY keyboard is currently the most widely available and utilized computer keyboard in most countries.

Conflicting stories surround the QWERTY layout's beginnings. One theory—possibly the most popular—is that the QWERTY keyboard layout was first created to make typing slower. In the past, pressing two adjacent keys quickly might cause a typewriter to jam. The QWERTY keyboard layout, on the other hand, made users type quicker because the keys did not stick as frequently. Another theory is that the pattern was developed through a number of trial-and-error layouts by early telegraph operators, according to the Smithsonian Institute. They discovered that translating morse code was made too difficult by the keys' initial alphabetical layout. They were finally able to type more quickly because to the QWERTY layout.

RAID

Any of the following may be referred to as RAID:

a. RAID, which stands for *redundant array of independent disks*, refers to a collection of hard drives that have been connected and configured in a specific way to assist safeguard or enhance the performance of a computer's disk storage. RAID is frequently utilized on servers and powerful computers. A device utilising RAID technology can be seen in the image of the Drobo. RAID employs a number of approaches, which are described below. Recall that RAID helps safeguard your data. RAID, however, shouldn't be used in place of a backup. RAID cannot be used to restore a file that has been deleted or overwritten.

Versions of RAID include:

- **RAID 0** - software stripping and block interleave versions (at least two drives). For speedier operation and a lower risk of overload, data is written to each drive in turn, with each block traveling to the next available drive (striping). Of course, the volume is not limited to the size of a single disk. Since no redundancy is offered, the system collapses if one drive fails. The quickest and most effective array type is RAID 0, however it has no fault tolerance.
- **RAID 1** - Duplexing and disk mirroring in RAID 1 (at least two drives). Data is written similarly to both drives when drives are used in pairs. By connecting to its own interface controller, each drive can be duplexed. One drive failing does not render the system unusable. Instead, the other drive keeps running. Of course, two drives are now required to provide

the same amount of storage as one drive. With this level, there is no performance improvement. The range of options for fault-tolerant, performance-critical settings. Furthermore, if fault tolerance is required for no more than two disks, RAID 1 is the sole option.

- **RAID 2** - Bit interleaving and data striping in RAID 2. One bit at a time, data is sequentially written to each drive. Data for checksums is stored on a different disk. Since ECC is included into nearly all contemporary disk drives, RAID 2 is highly sluggish when writing data to disk and is rarely utilized today.

- **RAID 3** - Bit interleaving and parity checking using data striping. Lever 2 is comparable to RAID 3, which is more dependable. One byte at a time, data striping is carried out across the drives. High data transfer rates are typically provided by using 4 or 5 disks. Parity data is stored on one drive exclusively. The parity drive can be used to rebuild the contents of the failed drive in the event of a single drive failure. Data writing is typically slower since each write operation requires accessing the parity disk. A problem arises when two or more drives fail. Long sequential records in data-intensive environments can be accelerated by using RAID 3. However, numerous I/O operations are not permitted.

- **RAID 4** - Parity checking and data striping are interspersed in RAID 4 blocks. Similar to level 3, RAID 4 employs block data striping similar to RAID 0 and a single parity disk. Each drive in this RAID level operates independently, each drive reading a block of data. Naturally, a controller failure would be disastrous. provides no advantages above RAID 5 and does not allow for multiple concurrent write operations.

- **RAID 5** - Block interleaving, data striping, and distributed check data on all drives are features of RAID 5. the one that NetWare should utilize. Distribution of parity information across all disks. As the number of disks rises, RAID 5 efficiency rises. Hot spares can be used to instantly rebuild a failing drive. The best option for multi-user scenarios where write performance is not a concern. However, RAID 5 arrays need at least three disks and more frequently, five drives.

- **RAID 6** - A log structured file system that adds a mapping between a disk drive's physical sectors and logical representation is part of RAID 6, an extension to RAID 5. Information is written in sequential physical disk sectors as it is being created.
- **RAID 10** - With the same failure tolerance as RAID 1, a RAID 10 Stripped array has segments that are RAID 1 arrays. Striping RAID 1 segments enables high I/O rates. RAID 1 is a good option for individuals who are thinking about it because it offers good write performance but is a costly solution.
- **RAID 53** - implemented as a striped RAID 0 array with RAID 3 arrays for each of its segments. The fault tolerance and overhead of RAID 3 are also present in RAID 53. RAID 3 is a great option for individuals who are thinking about it because it boosts write performance, but it is pricey and necessitates identical synchronization on all drives.

Random Access Memory (RAM)

The Random Access Memory (RAM) is part of the computer's Immediate Access Storage (IAS). Data, information and programs that the computer needs to perform particular tasks are held in the RAM. During the execution of any program (instructions), that particular program and the data which the program is supposed to process and transform into information, as well as the intermediate and final results of the processing is also stored in the RAM memory, until they are finally stored on disk, displayed on the screen or printed. Information stored in RAM is of a temporary nature. RAM is *volatile* memory. This means that when the computer is powered off, all the contents of the RAM is lost, unless it has been saved to a disk. .

Random File Organization

Records in a random file may appear to have been written in such a way that is unorderly (random). Nevertheless, random files are actually stored in a well-defined manner.

Range

Any of the following examples of a range would be:

a. A range often refers to *a number of numbers that fall between two other values*. The range between 1 and 5, for instance, is 2, 3, and 4.

b. In a spreadsheet, *a range or cell range* is a *collection of cells that are part of a row or column*. Columns A1 through A10, for instance, represent the range of cells that are combined together in the formula =sum(A1:A10). Given that all of the cells are present together, this form of range is known as an adjacent range. Each cell would have to be included in the formula if you wanted to include cells that were in a non-adjacent range. For instance, the cells A2, B2, and C2 are put together in the formula =sum(A2+B2+C2).

c. A range may be expressed by two (..) or three (...) periods in computer programming. For further details and examples, visit our page on ellipses.

Thus, in data validation, *a range is a group of values from a minimum to a maximum*. A range check validates data by ensuring that items fall in specified ranges or limits. In spreadsheets, a range is a series of cells that worked on as a group, and may refer to a row, column, or rectangular block defined by one corner and its opposite diagonally opposite corner.

Ransomware

Type of virus that blocks access to the victim's data and makes a ransom demand in exchange for not deleting or publishing it. Our ransomware prevention guide has more information.

Ransomware Attacks

The sophistication and frequency of ransomware assaults have considerably grown. In these attacks, data belonging to the victim is encrypted, and the hackers demand a ransom in return for the decryption key. Ransomware attacks have increased in recent years and frequently target important infrastructure and huge enterprises. Cybercriminals are also using "double extortion" strategies, in which they threaten to release the data they have stolen if the ransom is not paid.

Read

The *input of data from a peripheral device, such as a tape or disk into the computer.* The act of reading does not destroy what is read, and a read can be both input and output (I/O), since data is being output from the peripheral device and input into the computer.

Read/Write

In terms of primary memory, read/write is a feature exhibited by Random Access Memory (RAM) chips. Data can be read to and from the chip.

Read Only

In terms of primary storage, read only is a feature exhibited by the Read Only Memory (ROM) chips. Data is written on read only chips at the time of manufacture and can only be read and not altered by the user.

Read Only Memory (ROM)

Read only memory (ROM) is a memory chip that permanently stores data and instructions and forms a small portion of the computer's Immediate Access Storage (IAS). ROM storage is permanent. Its contents are placed into the ROM chip at the time of manufacture and cannot be altered. ROMs are used extensively to hold data and programs that are of a permanent nature. The computer's basic instructions that tell the processor how to carry out its functions (Operating system) are resident in the ROM chip. Random access memory is *non-volatile*. Its contents are of a permanent nature and cannot be lost when the computer is powered off.

Read Error

A read error *occurs when there is a failure to read data on a storage medium or memory device.* E.g., when magnetic or optical reading surfaces become contaminated with dust or dirt, or simply physically damaged, the bits may become indecipherable, or if there is a malfunction of one of the electronic components in a memory chip, the contents may be irretrievable.

Real-time

Real-time denotes *immediate response.* It is a system of processing of data or information at the time data is created. The term may also refer to fast transaction processing systems for business applications; though it is usually used to refer to process control applications, e.g. In air-line reservation systems.

Reboot

To *reload the operating system and start the computer.*

reCAPTCHA

A *CAPTCHA* that facilitates reading books in addition to protecting a website from bots or other scripts. In a *reCAPTCHA*, one word is generated by the script, while the other is a word that was scanned but couldn't be read by an OCR tool. The theory is that if a user comprehends one of the terms correctly, the other word must likewise be right.

The image is an illustration of a reCAPTCHA that asks for the words "were" and "tattoos" to be input in order to proceed. The word that is created and the word that is being scanned are unknown to reCAPTCHA.

Record

A *group of related fields* that are used to store data about a subject (master record) or activity (transaction record). A record can consist of different types of data e.g. numeric (such as Amount), while others can be non-numeric (such as Customer Name). A collection of records make up a file. *Master records* contain permanent data, such as Account number, and variable data such as Balance due. *Transaction records* contain permanent data such as quantity. A collection of records that are stored on a computer readable medium like diskettes is referred to as a *computer file.*

Refresh

To refresh *is to continuously charge a device that cannot hold its contents.* For example, dynamic memory chips (DRAMs) require constant refreshing to maintain their charged bit patterns.

Register

A term used to describe *a specific computer unit for storing a group of bits or characters.* It is *a small high-speed circuit that holds addresses and value of internal operations.* E.g., registers keep track of the address of the instruction being executed and the data being processed. When a program is debugged the contents of the registers may be displayed to determine the status of the computer at the moment of the failure.

Relational Database

A relational database is *a database that is perceived by its users as a collection of tables.* It is a method of organizing files in a database that does not allow repeating groups. All data value in a relational database is *atomic* i.e., at every row-and-column position in every table there is always one data value, never a set of values. The entire information content of the database is represented as *explicit data values,* and is the only method available in a relational database, as there are no *"links"* or pointes connecting one table to another. In non-relational systems (hierarchical, network) records in one file point to the locations of records in another, such as customers to orders, and vendors to purchases. In relational database, relationships between files are created by comparing data, such as customer numbers and names. A relational system can take ant two or more files and generate a new file from the records that meet the matching criteria.

Relative Address

A *number that is relative to the first location of the program rather than a fixed location of memory*. The relative address is added to the address in order to derive the absolute address, the actual current location of the data.

Relay

An *electrical switch that is used to allow a small current to control a larger one*. The small current energizes the relay, which then closes a gate, allowing the larger current to flow through.

Report Generator (same as *Report Writer*)

A *program for printing complete data processing reports, given only a description of the desired content and format of the output reports, and certain information concerning the input file*. It can either be a stand-alone program or can be part of a data base management system. It can be used to print only selected records from a file and sort them into a new sequence before printing.

Response Time

The time it takes the computer to respond to a user's request, such as, looking up a specific file.

Role-Based Access Control (RBAC)

RBAC streamlines access management and lowers the danger of over-privileged users by allocating rights based on preset roles. RBAC, commonly referred to as role-based security, is an access control technique that grants end users access depending on their roles inside your business. RBAC offers fine-grained control and is less error-prone than manually granting rights. It also offers a straightforward, controlled method to access management. This can lessen the risk of cyberattacks, safeguard sensitive data, and guarantee that employees can only access the data and take the activities necessary to execute their jobs. The least privilege principle governs this. Since access must be granted to hundreds or even thousands of employees depending on their positions and responsibilities, RBAC is popular in large enterprises. However, given that it is frequently simpler to handle than access, it is becoming more and more common among smaller firms.

Routine

A set of instructions that perform a specific task. Also called a *subroutine, function, procedure and module.*

Router

A router is a piece of hardware used to accept, examine, and transfer data to another network. The packets may also be dropped, converted to a different network interface, and used for other network-related operations. It's a *device that connects networks that use the same protocols together* and passes information among them.

Compared to *hubs and switches*, which can only carry out the most fundamental network operations, *routers have additional features*. A hub, for instance, can transmit data between computers or network devices but does not process or otherwise make use of the data. In contrast, routers have the ability to examine data delivered across a network, alter how it is packaged, and send it over or to another network. For instance, routers are frequently used in home networks to allow numerous computers to share a single Internet connection.

Router varieties include:

- *Wireless (Wi-Fi) Router* - Smartphones, computers, and other devices with Wi-Fi network capability can access the internet via wireless routers. Additionally, they might offer conventional Ethernet routing for a few wired network devices. Some Wi-Fi routers may transform an incoming internet signal from your ISP and function as a hybrid router and modem.
- *Brouter* - A networking device known as a *brouter,* sometimes

known as a bridge router, performs the functions of both a
bridge and a router.

- *Core Router* - A core router in a computer network is a router
  that only routes data within the network—it does not route
  data between networks.
- *Virtue Router* - In a VRRP configuration, a virtual router is
  employed as a backup router.

Run

To execute a computer program.

Sampling

Obtaining a value of a variable at regular or intermittent intervals.

SATA

SATA 1.0, which stands for *Serial ATA or Serial AT Attachment*, replaced the parallel ATA interface seen in IBM compatible computers when it was initially introduced in August 2001. Each drive in a disk array can receive performance at 1.5 Gbps (about 187 MBps) from SerialATA. It provides a thin, compact cable option and is backward-compatible with ATA and ATAPI (AT Attachment Packet Interface) devices, as shown in the "SATA Data Cable" image. Comparing this cable to the older ribbon cables used with ATA drives, it helps simplify cable routing and provides the machine with greater airflow.

eSATA interface - Through External SATA, often known as eSATA, SATA also supports external drives. eSATA provides many more benefits than alternative alternatives. It enables greater transfer speeds without bottlenecks like USB (universal serial bus) and FireWire, is hot-swappable, and supports disk drive technologies (such S.M.A.R.T).

However, there are certain drawbacks to eSATA, such as the fact that drives need an external power supply because eSATA does not distribute power through the cable like USB does. Additionally, the eSATA cable can be extended up to a maximum length of 2 meters. Don't expect eSATA to replace other external computer solutions due to these drawbacks.

Scareware

Type of cyber threat where a threat actor dupes the victim into believing that they unintentionally downloaded unlawful content or that their computer is afflicted with malware. The threat actor then presents the victim with a cure for the made-up issue, duping them into downloading and installing malware.

Scan

To sequentially search a file, examining it part by part.

Scanner

Scanners are *special input devices that allow the user to transfer photographs, images, or text from a printed source into the computer.* The scanner converts the printed image to an electronic form that the computer can use and that the operator can manipulate and store. Optical character readers (OCRs) are special scanners that recognize the shape of letters. They work by scanning printed text and the computer can read converting it electronically into data that. Use of an OCR can minimize the amount of direct input or re-keying that may be necessary when text is not yet in electronic form. Most low-cost scanners do not include OCR; the user is getting only an image of the text.

Thus, a scanner is a device that reads images, text and codes. The text and bar code scanners recognize printed fonts and bar codes and convert them into a digital code, such as ASCII. Graphics scanners convert a printed image into a video image (raster graphics) without recognizing the actual content of the actual text or pictures.

Sector

A *sector is the smallest unit of storage read or written by a computer.* Sectors are fixed in length, and the numbers of sectors usually reside in one track. However, hardware may vary the disk speed to fit more sectors into tracks located on the outer edges of the disk platter.

Secure Socket Layer (SSL) and Transport Layer Security (TLS)

These technologies encrypt data sent between clients and servers to protect online transactions and conversations. TLS and SSL are technologies that provide safe authentication and data transmission over the Internet. But how do TLS and SSL differ from one another?

TLS stands for Transport Layer Security, whereas SSL stands for Secure Socket Layer. The protocols used to ensure security between web browsers and web servers are Secure Socket Layer and Transport Layer Security. Secure Socket Layer (SSL) uses the message digest to construct a master secret and offers the fundamental security services of authentication and confidentiality, which is the major distinction between SSL and Transport Layer Security. While a master secret is created using a pseudo-random method in TLS (Transport Layer Security).

Sequential File Organization and Access

A *method of organizing data in a prescribed ascending or descending sequence.* Reading and comparing each record, starting from the beginning or end of the file, must search for data stored in this fashion. A *file is sequentially organized if all its records are organized in a particular logical sequence according to a key field* (e.g. student number in a student file). Sequential Access is a method of accessing records on a sequentially organized file, without using indexes. Records on a sequential file are organized in key field order. As such, since key fields are unique, special search methods; such as the *binary search*, can be used to locate records easily and quickly.

Serial File Organization and Access

The internal handling of data in a non-sequential fashion – one after another.

Serial Port

An external port on a computer that is used to connect a modem or other serial devices. A typical serial port uses a DB-25 or DB-9 connector.

Setup Program

A *program that configures a system for a particular environment.* In personal computers, this program is usually used to inform the operating of a major change, such as a new disk drive or VDU.

Server

A *server* is a piece of hardware or software that processes requests sent over a network and answers to them. A client is the device that submits a request and waits for a response from the server. The computer system that accepts requests for online files and transmits those files to the client is referred to as a "server" in the context of the Internet.

Network resources are managed by servers. A user might install a server, for instance, to handle print jobs, transmit and receive email, or host a website. They are very adept at doing complex calculations. Some servers—often referred to as dedicated servers—are devoted to a single project or website. However, a lot of servers today are shared servers that manage several websites, email, the DNS (domain name system), FTP, and DNS (domain name system).

Most servers are never shut off since they are frequently used to supply services that are continually needed. As a result, when servers malfunction, they can be quite problematic for both the firm and the network users. In order to address these problems, servers are frequently configured to be fault tolerant.

Simplex

One-way communication.

Single Sign-On (SSO)

One set of login information, such as a username and password, can be used by a user to access numerous applications thanks to single sign-on (SSO), a session and user authentication service. Enterprises, small and midsize businesses, and even individuals can utilize SSO to make managing various credentials easier. Users can log in to numerous applications using single sign-on without having to remember their passwords for each one separately.

Slave

A *computer or peripheral device that is controlled by another computer*. A terminal or computer in a remote location that only receives data is a typical example of a slave.

Smart Card

A *smart card is a credit card with a built-in microprocessor and memory that can be used as an Identity card or financial transaction card.* This makes it *smarter* than an ordinary credit card. The microprocessor and memory makes it possible for the smart card to store vital information about a client. When inserted into a card reader, the smart card transfers data to and from a central computer. Smart cards are now becoming a popular system of paying for goods and services without the use of actual cash. Smart cards are more secure than a magnetic stripe card and can be programmed to self-destruct if the wrong password is entered too many times. As a financial transaction card, it can store transactions and maintain a bank balance.

Smoke Test

A test of new or repaired equipment by turning it on. If there is smoke then it doesn't work.

Social Engineering Attacks

These strategies persuade victims to provide private data like passwords or credit card details. Phishing is a typical form of social engineering assault in which attackers pretend to be a reliable source in order to dupe victims into providing personal information. Attacks using social engineering pose significant difficulties since they target human weaknesses rather than technological ones.

Soft Copy

Refers to data displayed on a video display unit.

Software

A *set of instructions for the computer.* A series of instructions that performs a particular task is called a program or *software program.* The two major categories of software are *system software* and *application software.* System software is made up of control programs, including the operating system, communicating software and database manager. Application software is any program that processes data for the user.

Software House

An organization that specializes in developing customized software for a customer.

Software Package

An application program that has been developed for sale to the general public, and usually refers to off-the-shelf packages.

Software Publisher

An *organization that develops and markets software*. Software publishers do market research, development, production and distribution of software. The may develop their own software, contract for outside development or obtain software that has already been written.

Software as a Service (SaaS)

With software as a service, the service provider gives you a finished product that is operated and managed on your behalf. The majority of the time when software as a service is mentioned, end-user applications are meant. With a SaaS solution, you only need to consider how you will utilize that specific piece of software; you do not need to consider how the service is managed or how the underlying infrastructure is maintained. Web-based email is a typical example of a SaaS application since it allows you to send and receive emails without having to manage feature updates or upkeep for the servers and operating systems that the email program is using.

Sort

To *reorder data in a new sequence*. Sorting capabilities are provided within the operating system and many application programs, such as word processing and database management programs.

Source Code

A *program in its original form as written by the programmer*. Source code is not executable by the computer directly. It must be converted into machine language by compilers, assemblers and interpreters.

Spam

Any of the following may be considered spam:

- *Internet junk mail* is referred to as *spam* (not the meat product), also known as mass e-mail marketing, UCE (unsolicited commercial e-mail), and bulk e-mail. Spam is unsolicited email that is sent to tens of thousands or even millions of recipients with the purpose of promoting a specific good or service or a money-making fraud. Gary Thuerk, a Digital employee who was promoting the new DECSYSTEM-2020, 2020T, 2060, and 2060T on ARPANET, wrote the first spam email on May 1, 1978. Even though it's against the law in many nations, responding to spam might result in your email address being added to additional spam lists because it shows your address is active. It is typically preferable to not reply and delete any spam email that you receive. It's okay to click the Unsubscribe or Remove e-mail link if you're receiving spam from a business with which you gave your email address and you believe the business to be reliable.
- *Spam*, often referred to as flooding, occurs when many lines of the same text are posted more than once in a chat, forum, or newsgroup. When a message is placed in a newsgroup two or more times, it is often referred to as spam or a flood of messages.
- A person advertising a good or service is referred to as spam if they use any kind of internet communication.

Spaghetti Code

A *computer software program that is written without a coherent structure*. Each decision in a program directs the computer to branch to some other part of the program. Usually implies an excessive use of the GOTO instructions.

Spooling (Simultaneous Peripheral Operations On-line)

The *overlapping of low-speed operations with normal operations.* Today, spooling is usually used to buffer data for the printer as well as remote batch terminals. In the early days, spooling was used in mainframes to in order to optimize slow operations such as reading cards and printing. Card input was read onto disk and printer output was stored on disk.

Spyware

This software allows hostile actors to access data without authorization, including private information like payment information and login passwords. Mobile devices, desktop programs, and desktop browsers can all be impacted by spyware.

State-Of-The-Art

Refers to the most recent (latest) method or technique applied to designing and developing hardware and software.

Statement

In a high-level language, a statement is a descriptive phrase that generates one or more machine language instructions in the computer. In a low-level assembly language, programmers write instructions rather than statements, since each source language instruction is translated into one machine language instruction.

Start Bit and Stop Bit

In asynchronous transmission, a start bit is a bit transmitted before each character, while a stop bit is a bit transmitted after each character.

Storage Media

A *hardware unit that holds data.* It's a *device or portion of a device that is capable of receiving data, retaining it for an indefinite period of time, and supplying it on demand.* In this case we refer to external devices such as disks and tapes, in contrast with memory (RAM). A computer needs a place to keep its system software, other software applications, and data. Since RAM is only for temporary storage of programs and data while they are in use, the computer user must find another place for permanent storage.

"INFORMATION SYSTEMS UNRAVELED: EXPLORING THE CORE CONCEPTS"

There are two types of storage media: *floppy disks* and *hard disks*. The *floppy disk* is light and portable; it can be carried from machine to machine. Hard disks are built-in and cannot easily be moved from one machine to another. All CPUs have drives that read the information on the disks. All you can see of the floppy disk drives are the slots in the front of the computer. *Hard disk drives* are optional but most people choose to have them installed because of the extra storage they provide and because applications stored on hard drives usually run faster.

Floppy disks come in two sizes: 5.25 and 3.5 inches, although the smaller size is certainly the most popular now. They are enclosed in hard plastic so they are less subject to damage. *Floppy disks also have different densities*, which is the amount of data that can be stored on a disk. A low-density disk drive cannot read a high-density disk so this is an area of compatibility of which the user must be aware.

Hard drives come in increments of 100's of megabytes. (One megabyte is the rough equivalent of 700 pages of text.) Hard disk space is usually inexpensive and it not unusual for personal computers to have hard disk drives that offer more than 10,000 megabytes of storage. Other long-term storage media include removable cartridges and tape drives. These are usually used as back-up storage devices.

Streaming Tape

A high-speed magnetic tape drive that is frequently used to make a backup copy of an entire hard disk.

Straight Line Coding

Coding in which loops are avoided by the repetition of parts of the coding when required.

Structured Programming

A variety of *techniques that compels the programmer to use a logical structure on the writing of a program*. Large routines are broken down into smaller, more manageable modular routines. This programming methodology discourages the use of GOTO statements, which prevents a programmer from branching to a routine that does not ensure returning to the place in the program that called it. When documenting the *logical structure* of the program, certain programming statements are *indented*, so that the beginning and ending of each loop can easily be identified. Structured programming encourages peer programmers to offer constructive criticism of the programs through *structured walkthroughs*. Examples of *Structured languages* are like dBase and Pascal. *Unstructured languages* are such as COBOL, BASIC and FORTRAN.

Subroutine

A set of instructions necessary to direct the computer to carry out a well-defined mathematical or logical operation; a sub-unit of a routine. It is *a group of instructions to the computer that perform a specific function*, such as a function or macro. A large subroutine is usually called a *procedure* or a *module*, though these terms are used interchangeably.

Subschema

In database management, it is *an individual user's partial view of the whole database*. The entire database is called a schema.

Supercomputer

At present, *this is the fastest computer available*, and is mainly used in areas such as simulations in structural analysis, computational fluid dynamics, petroleum exploration and production, electronic design, physics and chemistry, meteorology, and nuclear energy research.

Switch

Any of the subsequent may be referred to as a switch:

- Each key on a computer keyboard has a *switch* underneath it that activates when the key is depressed. An example of a switch type used with laptop computers is the scissor switch. The illustration shows how a scissor switch works and how pressing the key compresses it.
- A *switch* is a physical component of circuitry that controls

signal flow. A switch or toggle switch enables the opening or closing of a connection. The switch permits a signal or power to pass through the connection when it is opened. The switch cuts the circuit connection and halts the flow when it is closed. Switches were used as a method of input by early computers like the Altair.

- In order to turn a gadget on or off, a switch might also be a button or lever.

- A *switch* is a hardware component that filters and forwards network packets on a network, although it typically isn't able to do much else. Compared to a hub, a network switch is more sophisticated, but not as sophisticated as a router.

- A command *switch* is an option that can be used in conjunction with a command when one is mentioned. For instance, the /MBR switch can be used with the command "fdisk". The user could build a new master boot record by using "FDISK /MBR".

Symbolic Coding

Instructions written in non-machine language.

Symbolic language

A *programming language that uses symbols, or mnemonics for expressions and operands.* All modern programming languages are symbolic languages.

Synchronous Data Transmission

A *data transmission method in which data is transmitted between the sending and the receiving computer at a constant rate, and there is no needs for start bits and stop bits between each character that has to be transmitted.* It is a format in which a block of contiguous data characters is transmitted without framing bits between characters. In synchronous data transmission, both stations are synchronized. Codes are sent from the transmitting station to the receiving station to establish the synchronization, and data is then transmitted in continuous steams. This method is faster than asynchronous transmission but is expensive and is mainly used where large volumes of data are to be transmitted at very high speeds.

Syntax

The *rules and regulations governing the structure of a language statement*, and specifies how words and symbols are put together to form a phrase.

Syntax Error

This type of error occurs when a program cannot understand the command that the user has entered.

System

An assembly of procedures, processes, methods, routines, techniques or equipment united by some form of regulated interaction to form an organized whole. A *computer system* comprises the CPU, operating system and some peripheral devices. An information *system* comprises the database, all the data entry, update, query and report programs and manual and machine procedures.

System Development Cycle

Refers to *the sequence of events in the development of an information system* (application), which must be adhered to by both the users and technical staff. The systems development cycle involves the following steps:

- **Systems analysis and design**
    - Feasibility study
    - General design
    - Prototyping
    - Detail design
    - Functional specification
- **User sign off**
- **Programming**

- ◦ Design
- ◦ Coding
- ◦ Testing
- **Implementation**
  - ◦ Training
  - ◦ Conversion
  - ◦ Installation
- **User acceptance**

Systems Development Methodology

Refers to the formal documentation for the phases of the system development cycle, and outlines clearly, the precise objectives of each phase and the results required from each phase before the next phase can start. Special forms are provided for the preparation of the documentation throughout each phase.

Systems Disk

Refers to the disk that contains part or all of the operating system or other control program.

System Failure

Refers to a hardware or software malfunction. System failure is usually associated with a problem within the operating system.

System File

A machine language file that is part of the operating system or some other control program, or may refer to a configuration file used by such programs.

System Flowchart

A pictorial diagram illustrating the flow of information into, through, and out of a system of programs.

System Life Cycle

The system life cycle is *the useful life of an information system*. The length of the life cycle depends on the nature and volatility of the business, as well as the software development tools used to generate the databases and application programs. An information system that is patched up many times over eventually loses its structural form and may not be expandable.

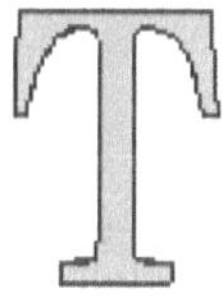

Table

A table is *a collection of adjacent fields*. It is also called an *array* and contains data that is either constant within the program or is called in when the program is run.

TCP/IP

TCP/IP, an acronym for *transmission control protocol and Internet protocol*, is a collection of guidelines (protocols) that regulates communications between all computers connected to the Internet. More specifically, TCP/IP specifies how data should be transferred, received, and packaged (into units of data known as packets) before being sent and received. By virtue of the efforts of Vint Cerf and Bob Kahn, TCP/IP was created in 1978.

TCP/IP, as its name suggests, *combines the Internet protocol (IP) and the transmission control protocol (TCP)*. The Internet Protocol standard specifies how packets are delivered over networks and provides instructions on their destination and route. Any computer connected to the Internet can advance a packet to a different computer that is one or more distances away from the intended recipient. It is comparable to a line of miners delivering pebbles from a quarry to a mining cart.

The Transmission Control Protocol is in charge of making sure that data is reliably transmitted across networks linked to the Internet. TCP examines packets for defects and submits retransmission requests if any are discovered.

Three TCP/IP protocols that are most widely used:

- **HTTP** - Used for insecure data exchanges between a web client and a web server. To see a web page, a web client—a computer's Internet browser—sends a request to a web server. Following receipt of this request, the web server notifies the web client of the web page information.

- **HTTPS** - is a secure data transfer protocol that is used between a web client and a web server. When transferring sensitive information to a web server from a web client (a computer's Internet browser), HTTPS is utilized.
- **FTP** - When connecting two or more computers, FTP is used. Direct communication between two computers allows for the transmission and reception of data.

Tag

In programming, a tag is a set of bits or characters that identifies various conditions about data in a file and is often found in the header records of such files. Also called *key fields* in a record.

Task Manager

Since Windows NT 4.0 and Windows 2000, the Task Manager has been a part of all Microsoft Windows operating systems. It enables you to see every task (process) running on the computer as well as its general performance. You can halt a frozen program, check the system resources that are available, and see how much memory a program is consuming by using the Task Manager. Think of the Task Manager as the Activity Monitor if you are more familiar with Apple machines.

Tailgating

Also Known As *Piggybacking* - is the act of a threat actor following authorized personnel inside a secured building. Usually, the staff member with authorized access holds the door open for the person in back because they believe they have permission to enter.

Teleconferencing

The act of holding a *conference call* or *meeting using phone lines or data communications connections* that are connected to several different places. Each participant in a teleconference must phone into the central location where the conference is being administered in order to connect with other callers.

Telnet

The *Internet standard protocol for remote terminal connection service used for logging into and searching other computers connected to the Internet*. Telnet allows your computer to interact with a remote timesharing system at another site as if your terminal were connected directly to the remote computer.

Terminal

In computing, a terminal is *an Input/Output (I/O) device* that usually uses the keyboard for input and a Video Display Unit (VDU) or printer for output.

Test Data

Refers to *a set of data created for testing new or revised programs, to determine the accuracy and adequacy of computer operation or system.* Test data should always be developed by the user in conjunction with the programmer and must contain a sample of every category of valid data as well as many invalid conditions.

Test Run

A test run *is performed when running new or revised programs to determine if they process all data properly*. The results of the run are compared with the correct results for this particular application.

Thrashing

An *undesirable situation in which computer systems using virtual memory become involved in excessive purging*. This situation arise when the operating system spends excessive amounts of time swapping program pages in and out of disk, when running programs that are not written to run in virtual memory environment.

Throughput

Refers to *the speed with which the computer can process data.* Therefore, a computer's throughput is a combination of its peripheral input output speeds, its internal processing speed, and the efficiency of its operating system and other system software all working together.

Time-Sharing

Refers to *a computer environment whereby several authorized users are allowed to gain access to selected programs or databases.* This means that, although the computer actually services each user in sequence, the high speed at which the computer operates makes it appear as though the users are all being handled simultaneously.

Top-Down Design

Top down design is a design technique in which the designer starts with highest level of an idea and works its way down to the lowest level of detail.

Top-Down Programming

A programming design and documentation technique that imposes a hierarchical structure on the design of the program. See *structured programming.*

Topology

A *method for interconnecting individual workstations in a local area network.* Three popular topologies are bus, star, and ring.

Track

A *portion of a moving storage medium such as a disk or drum that is accessible to a given reading station.* On magnetic disks, tracks are concentric circles (data storage) or spirals (CDs and Videodiscs). On tapes, tracks are parallel lines. The format of the tracks is determined by the specific drive they are used in. On magnetic devices, data bits are recorded as reversals of polarity in the magnetic surface. On CDs, data bits are recorded as physical pits underneath a clear, protective layer.

Trailer

In data processing, a trailer *is the last record in a file,* which usually contains the number of records in the file and hash total.

Transaction

Transactions are *activities that occur or requests made by the user* and are reflected on a file. *Transactions* that are recorded in a business environment include orders, purchases, additions and deletions, and changes. Queries and other requests are also transactions to the computer, though they are usually acted upon and not recorded in the transaction file. The *volume of transactions in an organization usually determines the size and speed of a computer system.*

Transaction File

A transaction file is *a collection of records that record the activity of an organization.* The data stored in the master file; which contains the subject of the organization, is updated using data collected in the transaction file. Transaction files are usually transferred from the active disk files to the data library after a period of time, and serve as audit trails.

Transaction Processing

Transaction processing is a terminology that describes *the processing of transactions as they are received by the system.* Transaction processing systems are also called *on-line systems* or *real-time systems.* They update the master files as soon as transactions are entered at the terminals or arrive via communication lines. Transaction processing systems differ from *batch processing,* which stores transactions and updates the necessary files at a later date.

Transmission

Refers to the transfer of data over a communication channel.

Trap

In programming, to trap is to test for a particular condition in a running program. *Error traps* test for error conditions and provide specific routines for error recovery. *Debugging traps* tests for the execution of a particular instruction. Traps can test for specific hardware interrupts to cause a special routine to be activated.

Trojan

Type of viruses which deceive users into believing they are dealing with a harmless file. A Trojan can attack a system and create a backdoor that can be used by attackers.

Trunk

A trunk is *a communications channel between two nodes or points*. This terminology is commonly used with telephone systems and usually refers to large bandwidth channels between major switching centers, which are capable of transmitting many simultaneous voice conversations or data signals.

Turn-Around Document

A turn-around document is *a document that is initially printed by the computer, and later used as an input document to the computer*. It is a paper document or punched card that is prepared in such a way that it will be re-entered into the computer system. Paper documents are printed with special fonts for optical scanning, and punched cards are punched with appropriate codes. Examples of turn-around documents are invoices, inventory stock cards and multiple-choice type of examination papers prepared for optical scanning.

Turnkey System

Refers to *a complete system of hardware and software delivered to the customer in a ready-to-run state*. Turnkey system usually has all the necessary software installed and ready to run.

Twisted Pair Cable

A low bandwidth connecting cable used in telephone systems. The cable has two insulated wires that are wrapped around each other to minimize interference from other wires.

T1

A T1 is a *leased data communication line* with a 1,544,000 bit per second transmission rate. T1 lines are used to connect to an ISP or to send network data from a business to the Internet.

The following advantages of "T-Carrier" (T1 lines):

- Because lines are synchronous, your download and upload speeds are the same.
- Since lines are dedicated, you won't be sharing your connection with anybody else.

- It's a more secure connection as it's a dedicated line.
- Despite all of these lines' advantages, competing options like fiber optic lines are starting to gain favor due to the demand for additional bandwidth.

T2

T2 is a *leased data communication line* with a 6.3 megabit per second transmission rate.

The following are a few advantages of "T-Carrier" (T2 lines):

- Since lines are dedicated, you won't be sharing your connection with anybody else.
- It's a more secure connection as it's a dedicated line.
- Because lines are synchronous, your download and upload speeds are the same.
- Despite all the advantages of conventional lines, fiber optic lines are gaining popularity as an alternative because of the demand for additional bandwidth.

T3

A T3 is a *leased data communication line*, also known as a *DS3 (Digital Signal 3)*, that can send a digital signal at a speed of 44.746 megabits per second. They were initially created by Bell Labs and are utilized by businesses that need a backbone or medium levels of bandwidth. Coaxial cable measuring 75 ohms is used in the cable, and BNC connectors are used for connection.

T3 is still fast enough, but as fiber optic connections become available, many are switching because of their extremely rapid upload and download rates.

T3 line characteristics

- Since lines are dedicated, you won't be sharing your connection with anybody else.

- It's a more secure connection as it's a dedicated line.
- Because lines are synchronous, your download and upload speeds are the same.

Unbundled

Refers to the separation of prices for each component in a system.

Unconditional Branch

In computer programming, it is *a branching instruction that passes control from one part to another part of the program unconditionally.* E.g. a GOTO, JUMP or BRANCH instruction.

Uninterruptible Power Supplies (UPS)

Uninterruptible power supplies are devices that insure a steady and clean supply of electricity to a computer. A sudden loss of or change in power can destroy data and cause damage to a computer. UPSs give the user time to exit from all active applications and save all current data in the event of a power outage. Many computers have some internal protection against power surges. Users can also plug their equipment into surge-protector power strips. Only a UPS, however, offers standby power if there is a power outage. A UPS is a sophisticated battery that augments power or compensates for sudden losses in electric flow.

UNIX

An operating system for a wide variety of computers, from mainframes to personal computers. It supports multi-tasking and is suited to multi-user environments (see *Operating Systems*).

Update

Updating refers to the *process of changing the data in the file or database so that the file or database contains the latest data/information.* During update all affected records are searched for and then amended (updated) to reflect the latest situation. Update implies adding and deleting records in files.

URL

A URL (*Uniform Resource Locator*), also referred to as an internet address or web address, is a defined naming convention and URI (uniform resource identifier) for addressing documents accessible over the Internet and Intranet. A computer can find and open a web page on another computer through the Internet thanks to the URL. The website address **https://www.patwest-zambia.com** is an illustration of a URL.

The browser is informed via the **HTTP** (*Hypertext Transfer Protocol*) which protocol is used to access the data given in the domain. *"Hypertext Transfer Protocol Secure"* is the abbreviation for a "**HTTPS**" protocol, which denotes that data being communicated over HTTP is encrypted and secure. The colon (:) and two forward slashes (//) that follow the HTTP or HTTPS divide the protocol from the rest of the URL.

User

A user is *any individual who interacts with a computer at an application level.* Programmers, operators, and other technical staff are not considered as users when working in a professional capacity on a computer.

User Interface

A user interface refers to *a combination of menus, screen design, keyboard commands, command language and help screens, which together create a user interacts with the computer.* User interface may also include devices such as a mouse, and touch screen. A well-defined user interface is crucial to the success of a software package as it makes it *user-friendly.*

Utility program

Refers to a *program that supports the operations of a computer.* Utility programs provide file management capabilities, such as searching, copying, comparing, sorting and listing, as well as diagnostic and measurement routines that check the health and performance of the computer system.

Validity

In programming, validity refers to the *correctness*; capable of measuring, predicting, or representing according to intention or design. Validity checking refers to a set of routines in a data entry program that tests the input for the correct and reasonable conditions, such as numbers falling within a given range, or correct spelling.

Validation

Before any data is admitted into a computer system, it must first be validated or verified. This procedure aids in preventing data breach or transmission-related corruption. Incoming data must be exact, complete, and correct ("*valid*") before it can be used. A poor analysis or processing of the data could be caused by incorrect or insufficient ("*invalid*") data. All analyses conducted on the complete data set may be flawed if some data is invalid.

The software application must be able to recognize errors when users enter data incorrectly and prompt the user to make the necessary corrections.

Incorrect data should never be sent to the software's data processing procedures if the user purposefully entered it incorrectly. When data is accidentally corrupted during storage or transmission, data validation can also identify it.

The following are typical generic types of data validation carried out by software programs:

- *Format Validation* - Verifies that the data is submitted in the appropriate format through format validation. An application might, for instance, request that the user enter a date in the format MM-DD-YYYY (two-digit month, followed by a dash, two-digit day, followed by another dash, and four-digit year). To make sure the amount of characters and the location of the dashes adhere to that format, it is important to double-check the user's input data.

- *Code Validation:* This process verifies that any encoded data complies with the code standard. No matter how simple or complicated a coding system is, this type of validation can be used on it. If a user is asked to enter a postal code into an application, the accuracy of the input should be checked by comparing it to a table of real-world postal codes. An application should validate input in accordance with the relevant XML standard if it takes XML data as input. *Data Type Validation* - Verifies the input's data type via data type validation. After confirming the format, the characters in the date example above, for instance, should be examined to ensure that they are numeric.

- *Range Validation* - Validates that the numbers are within a certain range. For instance, all numeric numbers in the date sample above should be higher than zero. Given that there are only 12 months in a year, the month value should always be smaller than 13. The day value must never be greater than 32. The day value should never be larger than 29 if the month value is 2 (for "February"). The day value shouldn't be more than 28 if the month value is 2 and the year value modulo 4 equals zero, indicating a leap year.

- *Consistency Validation* - Validates consistency by checking if the data is logically consistent with the input that was requested in relation to other data. For instance, if a form requests a date of birth, it should obviously be a recent date.

- *Validation Of Uniqueness* – Verifies, if necessary, that the data is unique. For instance, if you ask the user to choose a username, it needs to be different from any others already in use.

Variable

In programming, a variable is *a structure that holds data and is given a unique, and usually meaningful name by the programmer*. A variable holds data assigned to it until a new value has been assigned to it or until the program is finished.

Variables are used to hold values. E.g. A simple statement in C programming language: **for (a=0; a<10; a++), a** is a *variable* that is initially set to zero **(a=0)**, incremented **(a++),** and tested ten times **(a<10)** to perform an operation. Variable are used to hold items of data temporarily while they are being processed. Variables are usually assigned with an equal sign; for example, month = **2**, places a 2 in the variable called "month". Unquoted data is used for numeric data; e.g. **Month = 1,** while character data requires quotes: **name = "Morris".** A *local variable* **is** one that can be referenced only within the subroutine, function or procedure it was defined in, while the entire program can use a global variable.

Variable Length Field

A variable length field is a term used to describe *a record structure that holds fields of varying lengths.* There is more programming with variable length fields, because every record has to be separated into fixed length fields after it is brought into memory. Subsequently, each record has to be coded into the variable length format before it can be written to disk. For example, a customer name JOHN DEER would take up nine bytes and ANTHONY VAN KORP would take up 16 bytes of memory. One or two bytes of control information may be added. This implies that if fixed length fields were used in this example, 16 bytes or more would have to be reserved for every name. Compressing data on its way to the disk, and decompressing it when it comes back can achieve these same storage savings. This way, all the blank spaces in fixed length fields will be filtered out; however, unless this method is integrated into the operating system, it may provide unacceptable performance.

Variable Length Record

A variable length record is a record that contains one or more variable length fields.

Verification

In data entry operations, verification simply means to compare the keystrokes of a second operator with the files created by the first operator.

Verifier Operator

Verifier operators are members of the data processing department and are *responsible for data verification after data entry operators have keyed data in*. When data has been keyed in completely, the data preparation operators can exchange their key stations in such a way that data preparation operator **X** goes to occupy the key station that data preparation operator **Y** was using, and vice versa. This is to enable the operators verify each other's work and thus lessen the number of errors in the data being prepared for entry. Usually, the key stations are switched to verify mode, in which case the verifier operator simply keys in the same data that the previous operator keyed in. As the verifier operator keys in the data, the system compares the same data that was keyed in by the previous operator to the one being entered by the verifier operator. If the two sets of data matches (meaning the data is valid) the system permits the verifier operator to continue keying in more data. If on the other hand there is a mismatch, the verifier operator. If there is a mismatch (meaning there are errors), the system will notify the verifier operator who is expected to verify with the source documents and the correct the error(s). This process continues until all the data has been verified and certified error free.

Video Graphics Array (VGA)

An *analog monitor that displays as many as 256 colors simultaneously*, with a resolution of 640 pixels horizontally and 480 lines vertically. (See Monitor).

View

To view is basically *to display and look on the screen*. In relational database management, a view is *a special display of data that is created as needed*. Typically, a view combines two or more files together so that the combined files can be displayed, printed or queried, e.g. customers and orders can be linked. All the fields to be included are specified by the user. The original files are not permanently linked or altered; but if the system allows the viewed data to be directly edited, the data in the original files will be changed.

Virtual LANs (VLANs)

A virtual LAN (VLAN) is a logical overlay network that isolates the traffic for each group of devices that share a physical LAN. A LAN is a collection of computers or other devices that are connected to the same physical network and are located in the same location, such as the same campus or building. By dividing various user groups and traffic kinds, VLANs enable separated network segments within a physical network, improving security.

Virtual Memory

Virtual memory is *a technique that simulates more memory than actually exists and allows the computer to run several programs concurrently regardless of their size*. In this technique, each program run on the computer is divided into segments called *pages*. The entire program is then stored on some direct access medium and the pages of the program are called into memory, as they are needed for execution. , thereby overlaying the page still in memory. If a memory page contains variable or other data that are altered by the running of the program, the page is temporarily stored on a disk when room is needed for new pages. The input and output of program pages is called *paging* or *swapping*. *Thrashing* occurs when unstructured programs are run in virtual memory, which is an excessive amount of disk access to bring in program segments. Disk access should be reserved for calling in the next set of data, not the same instructions again and again (as is the case with programs that contain a lot of spaghetti codes).

Virtual Private Networks (VPNs)

A virtual private network (VPN) is a method for establishing a secure connection over an unsecured communication channel, like the public Internet, between a computing device and a computer network or between two networks. In order to allow users of a private network (one that prohibits or restricts public access) to send and receive data over public networks as if their devices were directly linked to the private network, a VPN can extend private networks. Security, lower expenses for dedicated connection lines, and more flexibility for remote workers are all advantages of a VPN. VPNs can also be used to get around internet filtering. Although not a fundamental component of a VPN connection, encryption is frequently used. By establishing a virtual point-to-point connection over existing networks using tunneling technologies, a VPN is built. Some of the advantages of a wide area network (WAN) can be obtained using a VPN that is accessible via the open Internet. The resources accessible within the private network can be accessed remotely from the user's perspective. VPNs create encrypted tunnels for secure communication over open networks, preserving the integrity and confidentiality of data.

Virus

A harmful software, script, macro, or piece of code known as a computer virus is made to harm your computer, steal your personal information, alter data, send emails, show messages, or do a combination of these things.

When the virus is run, it replicates itself inside or on top of data files, applications, the boot sector of the hard drive, and anything else that may be written to. Writers gain access to a host machine through social engineering, zero-day vulnerabilities, or other methods, in order to spread the virus.

Computer viruses and other malware can infect a computer in a variety of ways. Shareware, pirated software, email, P2P programs, and other platforms where users share data are common ways that viruses are spread. If the infected program is executed after being downloaded, copied, or otherwise acquired, it might have an impact on anything that a computer can access.

By using an antivirus protection tool, you can shield your computer against infections. An antivirus program searches for virus signatures after being installed on a computer to monitor, identify, and remove any computer infections. It is advised to use an antivirus or antimalware protection tool to find and remove any computer viruses or other malware from the computer.

Virus types affect what they can do to a machine. The majority of computer viruses alter other files on the computer, overwrite data, display messages, and erase data. Virtually all computer viruses only harm the computer's data; they do not harm the machine's hardware. For instance, a non-resident virus can infect a particular file and, when that file is opened, spread to other files, corrupting and erasing them.

Vishing

Voice Phishing (also known as *Vishing*) assaults use social engineering strategies to coerce victims into divulging financial or personal information over the phone.

Voice Recognition

Voice recognition, often known as speech recognition, refers to a piece of technology or software that can recognize human speech. Voice recognition software is frequently used to control a device, issue commands, or write without the need for a keyboard, mouse, or button presses. Today, automated speech recognition (ASR) software applications are used to perform this on a computer. To improve the quality of the speech-to-text conversion, many ASR applications ask the user to "train" the machine to identify their voice. Saying "open Internet" for instance would cause the computer to launch the web browser.

You need a computer with a sound card, a microphone, and either a headset or a microphone for voice recognition to function. Other gadgets, like smartphones, come with all the required hardware already installed. Additionally, the software you use must support voice recognition, or you must install an application like Nuance Naturally Speaking if you want to utilize speech recognition everywhere.

Volatile Memory

The term *Volatile memory refers to memory that does not hold its contents without power*, such as a computer's main memory, made up of dynamic Random Access Memory (RAM) or static RAM chips, loses its contents immediately power is switched off. Therefore, it is advisable to save your work onto a disk every 15 – 20 minutes when you are typing a large document on your computer. This will reduce the likelihood of losing a large amount of data in case of a power failure. Where possible, the use of an Un-interruptible Power Supply Unit (UPS) is recommended.

Volatility

As a characteristic associated with data files, *volatility refers to a measure of the frequency at which records are added to the file or deleted from the file during a given period of time*. A file *volatile* if the records it contains are often added to or removed from the file. A *static file*, also called *non-volatile* file is one whose records do not change.

"INFORMATION SYSTEMS UNRAVELED: EXPLORING THE CORE CONCEPTS"

WAIS

WAIS is an acronym for *Wide Area Information Servers*. It is another type of search engine for the Internet. WAIS (pronounced "ways") is more powerful than gopher because it actually searches the full text of a document to look for specified key words. WAIS accepts commands in plain English, processes them at the user level, and relays the processed information from the user to the selected databases. There are many libraries on the Internet that have been set up to provide free access to documents and other resources. The documents stored on these WAIS servers are indexed (usually by every word in the document). In response to your query, WAIS searches the index on the server or servers you specified and tells you which documents are likely to hold information you're searching for. WAIS servers can be good sources of information on science-related topics.

WPA and **WPA2**

These protocols increase the security of wireless networks by encrypting data and authenticating users. The Wi-Fi Alliance developed **Wi-Fi Protected Access (WPA)** as a direct response to the WEP standard's growing number of flaws. A year before WEP was legally phased out, in 2003, WPA was officially adopted. The WPA-PSK (Pre-Shared Key) configuration is the most popular. WPA uses 256-bit keys, which is a substantial improvement over the WEP system's usage of 64-bit and 128-bit keys.

WPA introduced some significant changes, including as the Temporal Key Integrity Protocol (TKIP) and message integrity checks (to see if an attacker had intercepted or manipulated packets sent between the access point and client). Compared to the fixed key system used by WEP, the per-packet key scheme employed by TKIP is far more secure.

The Advanced Encryption Standard (AES) eventually replaced the TKIP encryption standard. WPA2 has officially taken the place of

WPA as of 2006. The requirement for AES algorithms and the addition of CCMP (Counter Cipher Mode with Block Chaining Message Authentication Code Protocol) as a replacement for TKIP are two of the biggest differences between WPA and WPA2. But TKIP is still kept in WPA2 as a backup method and for compatibility with WPA. The main security flaw in the WPA2 system is currently a difficult-to-find one (and necessitates the attacker's prior access to the encrypted Wi-Fi network in order to obtain specific keys and afterwards continue an attack against other devices on the network). Because of this, the known WPA2 vulnerabilities have nearly exclusively negative security implications for enterprise.

Whaling

Is a phishing scheme, prominent workers are the intended targets (whales), such as the CEO or CFO. By using deception, the threat actor tries to induce the victim to reveal sensitive information.

Wide – Area Network (WAN)

A method of connecting computers, peripherals, and communications equipment within a very large area. WANs can connect computers from organizations all over the world.

Window

A rectangular, on-screen frame through which you can view a document, worksheet, or other application.

WINDOWS

A windowing environment and application program interface for MS-DOS that brings to IBM compatible computers some of the graphical user interface features of the Macintosh computers.

Wireless Intrusion Detection Systems (WIDS)

A Wireless Intrusion Detection System (WIDS) is a security tool used to keep track of and guard against unauthorized access, malicious activity, and other security risks on wireless networks. Its primary goal is to spot suspect or unauthorized wireless activity and notify network managers in order to protect the network's confidentiality, integrity, and availability. To track and analyse wireless traffic, a WIDS typically consists of sensors or access points deployed strategically throughout the network architecture. These sensors pick up wireless signals and inspect them for indications of unauthorized gadgets, rogue access points, network intrusions, or rules violations. A WIDS's main goal is to identify and address security incidents in real-time or almost real-time.

Word

A word is *the computer's internal storage unit and refers to the amount of data it can hold in its registers and process at one time.* E.g. A 32-bit computer processes four bytes in the same time an 8-bit computer processes one byte, as long as the timing clocks are of equal speed.

Word Processor

The single most universal application for personal computers. Word processing programs convert computers into writing and editing machines. Word processing easily allows revisions, formatting, and corrections.

Worms

Worms are a type of malware that are made to use backdoors and vulnerabilities to infiltrate operating systems without authorization. The worm can launch numerous assaults after installation, including Distributed Denial of Service (DDoS).

WYSIWYG

Pronounced *'wizzy-wig'*, an acronym for *What You See is What You Get*. A term used in desktop publishing that means that - What you see on the computer screen is exactly what you get on paper when you print.

Workstation

A workstation is *a high-performance, single user microcomputer,* which the user operates. In a local area network (LAN) a workstation is a personal computer, which is connected to the network using a Network Interface Card (NIC). A workstation can also have its own operating system such as DOS, and may not have a floppy disk drive.

World Wide Web (WWW)

The most powerful search tool, WWW is a tool for working with collections of data, or databases. *It is a hypertext-based system that provides access to a variety of files and information.* Hypertext allows a user doing research on one document to jump to a related item in another document through hypertext links. WWW was originally developed at CERN (the European Particle Physics Laboratory in Geneva, Switzerland).

In WWW, each document contains highlighted items for which additional information is available. The additional information is contained in another document that is displayed when the user selects the highlighted item. With appropriate software, such as Mosaic or Netscape, the user can view not just text but pictures, sound files, and video.

Z

226

Zero Trust Architecture

The phrase "zero trust" (ZT) refers to a growing body of cybersecurity concepts that shift the focus of defences away from network-based perimeters and toward users, assets, and resources. The industrial and enterprise infrastructure and workflows are planned using zero trust concepts in a zero trust architecture (ZTA). Zero trust presupposes that there is no implicit trust given to assets or user accounts based only on their geographic or network location (for example, local area networks as opposed to the internet) or on the type of ownership of the asset (for example, corporate or private ownership).

Before a session to an enterprise resource is established, authentication and authorization (on the part of both the subject and the device) are separate tasks carried out. The enterprise network trends of distant users, BYOD, and cloud-based assets have prompted the concept of zero trust. Zero Trust architecture is based on the idea that no user or device should be automatically trusted, necessitating ongoing authentication and access controls. Organizations today require a new security paradigm that more successfully responds to the complexity of the contemporary workplace, welcomes the hybrid office, and safeguards users, devices, apps, and data wherever they may be.

References

1. Bunzel, M.J. and S.K. Morris, (1992). 'Multimedia Applications Development', McGraw Hill, Inc., New York.
2. Pujari, A.K., (1991). 'Nonmonotomic reasoning for image understanding', in Artificial Intelligence and Expert System Technologies [Ed] VVS Sarma et al. Tata McGraw-Hill

Don't miss out!

Visit the website below and you can sign up to receive emails whenever Patrick Mukosha publishes a new book. There's no charge and no obligation.

https://books2read.com/r/B-A-HJNZ-FVJPC

BOOKS2READ

Connecting independent readers to independent writers.

Did you love *"Information Systems Unraveled: Exploring the Core Concepts"*? Then you should read *"Exploring Computer Systems: From Fundamentals to Advanced Concepts"*[1] by Patrick Mukosha!

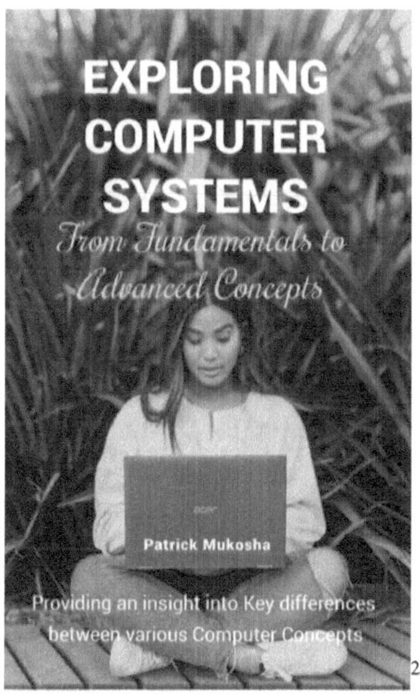

The essential manual "Exploring Computer Systems: From Fundamentals to Advanced Concepts" takes readers on a thorough tour of the world of computer systems. This book offers a thorough examination of computer systems, starting with the fundamentals and advancing to complex concepts.

The book's excellent basis in computer architecture and components at the outset makes it understandable for both newcomers and seasoned IT experts. The basic concepts of hardware, software, and their relationships are covered, enabling readers to comprehend how contemporary computer systems operate within.

---

1. https://books2read.com/u/bzBBxG

2. https://books2read.com/u/bzBBxG

Readers delve into the complexities of operating systems, including as process management, memory management, and file systems, as they move through the chapters. The author is succinct and straightforward. These complicated subjects are demystified by the author's succinct and simple explanations, making them understandable to readers of all skill levels.

This book's covering on networking and communication protocols is one of its best qualities. It offers a thorough review of computer networking and communication in local and wide-area networks, illuminating terms like TCP/IP, routing, and security. The fascinating worlds of virtualization and cloud computing are also highlighted in the book. The impact of virtual machines and cloud services, which have transformed the IT environment and increased computing flexibility, scalability, and affordability, is explained to readers.

Also by Patrick Mukosha

GoodMan
Resilient Strategies: Thriving in Harsh Business Conditions
Strategic Entrepreneurship: Navigating The Path To Success
Decisive Power: Navigating How to Make Toughest Decisions
"Reigning the Boardroom: A Trailblazing Guide to Corporate
Governance Success"
Fortifying Digital Fortress: A Comprehensive Guide to Information
Systems Security
"Unleashing the Power of Inclusive Innovation: Transforming the
World for All"
"Exploring Computer Systems: From Fundamentals to Advanced
Concepts"
"Computer Viruses Unveiled: Types, Trends and Mitigation
Strategies"
"The Pinnacle of Success: Unveiling the World's 20 Most Successful
Brands in 2023"
"Mastering Relational Databases: From Fundamentals to Advanced
Concepts"
"Navigating Change: A Comprehensive Guide to Change
Management"
"Information Systems Unraveled: Exploring the Core Concepts"

About the Author

Patrick Mukosha is a Management Consultant originally from Kitwe, Copperbelt Province of Zambia. He has a Doctorate in Management (Strategic Management) and Masters (Strategic Planning) from Atlantic International University, USA. He also holds a bachelor's in Information Technology from University of East Anglia, Norwich, UK, and a Diploma in Business Management from Canterbury College of Technology, Canterbury, UK. Member of the Institute for Leadership Development, York University, USA (2001–08), He was elected Vice President-Midlands of Computer Society of Zambia (2004), Executive Director for VISION-2011 – a consortium of NGOs (2009 – 2011, Founder of Strategic Management Community of Zambia (2017), Vice Chairperson Mungule Ward Development Committee (2021-2026). He has worked for more than 15 years for International IT and Telecommunication companies in senior management portfolios. After finishing his PhD in 2017, he embarked on career as a Management Consultant. He has worked on several Strategic Planning projects and conducts coaching and mentorship in Entrepreneurship, Business Management, Strategic Management and ICT. He's an aggressive serial entrepreneur and founder of PatWest Technologies.